Table of Con

- 1.1. Introduction of Slow Cooker
- 1.2. Design and Operation   5
- 1.3. Maintenance and Care   7
- 1.4. Advantages   9
- 1.5. Disadvantages   10
- 1.6. Cooking Tips   11

2.1. Recipes

1. Slow Cooked Chicken Tikka Masala   13
2. Chicken with Mushrooms and Bacon   15
3. Soy Braised Chicken   17
4. Jalapeno chicken   19
5. Angel Chicken   21
6. Chicken, Shrimp Jambalaya   23
7. Coq Au Vin   25
8. Sweet, sour and saucy chicken   27
9. Cranberry Chicken   29
10. Cashew Chicken   31
11. Chicken Cacciatore   33
12. Chicken Sloppy Joe   35
13. Cheesy Chicken with Penne Pasta   37
14. Italian tangy chicken with Artichokes   39
15. Chicken Noodles Alfredo   41
16. Spiced slow-cooked Beef Sloppy Joes   43
17. Beer Braised Beef Ribs   45
18. Slow cooked Beef Goulash   47
19. Slow Cooked Beef Lo Mein   49

20. Corned Beef with Orange-spice   51
21. Slow cooked Beef and Stout Casserole   53
22. Beef and Carrot Ragout   55
23. Slow cooked Massaman Beef Curry   57
24. Balsamic Pork Tenderloin   59
25. Pork and Mushroom Ragout   61
26. Country style pork tenderloin in gravy   63
27. Slow cooked Pork Carnitas   65
28. Slow cooked pork with Apple cider   67
29. Island Pork Roast   69
30. Slow cooker Chicken Pot Roast   71
31. Italian style Beef roast   73
32. German style Beef roast with veggies   75
33. Duck Ragu with Pappardelle   77
34. Nachos with Shredded Beef   79
35. Greek Lamb with Orzo   82
36. Beef and Bean Tortilla   84
37. Shredded Beef Barbeque   86
38. Slow cooked Beef Stroganoff with crunchy onion   88
39. Smoky Beef Brisket Tacos with Shredded Cabbage   90
40. Asian Beef curry   92
41. Slow cooked Round Steak   94
42. Balsamic Glaze Roasted Beef Tenderloin   96
43. Thit heo kho tieu   99
44. Slow Cooker Mediterranean beef roast   101
45. Slow cooker Beef Au jus   103
46. Pork and beef meatballs with Rigatoni Pasta   105

Other Best-Sellers from this Author:

1.1. Introduction of Slow Cooker:

Slow cooker or Crock-pot is just another electric cooking appliance that can cook healthy and delicious food. However, the most interesting feature of this cooking appliance is that it offers almost fully unattended cooking. Most importantly, with a slow cooker handy, you can expect a freshly cooked, warm meal waiting for you in the kitchen when you come back from office or when you wake up in the morning. It surely sounds amazing, doesn't it?

Slow cooker has a few truly amazing features that can make this possible for you. It has a timer that can be set in advance according to the cooking process needed for a dish. Few models of slow cooker even come with software installed in it with which you can program the sequences of cooking process and be worry free. Slow cooking needs a very little preparation time from your side. For example: You can arrange the ingredients in the cooker pot and program the settings and turn it on just before you are going to sleep or leaving for office. All the rest will be taken care by the slow cooker. It will keep cooking for hours, without allowing the food to burn and it's safe to use in any household. It is good for making soups, stews, boiled meals and also for baking, frying etc.

In short, you can cook almost everything in it. It cooks with low heat setting, provides uniform heating and keeps the food warm for hours. This concept of using slow cooker for making meals is particularly popular in US, Canada, New Zealand and Australia, however, its popularity and the flavor of its goodness is spreading throughout the world slowly and it is predicted that it is going to be the most admired and popular cooking style of the current century.

1.2. Design and Operation:

It is an oval or round lidded pot made with porcelain or glazed ceramic. A metal wire surrounds it through which heat can be generated with electrical charges. The lid is generally made of glass and placed on the grooved edge of the pot. Vapor concentrates in the groove and creates a mild atmospheric pressure outside of the pot, which in turn, balances the water vapor pressure created inside the pot. This eliminates the chance of any sudden release of vapor. This pressure balance mechanism makes this cooker different and safer from the regular pressure cooker.

The main cooking area, the pot or the ceramic vessel is designed in such way that it can maintain steady heat. The capacity of the pot may vary from 500 ml (16 oz) to 7 liters (7.4 US quarts). There is a liquid level indicator which is to protect the cooker from uncontrolled heating. The recommended liquid level should be maintained always for safety.

Generally, a slow cooker has two or more temperature settings levels like, 'low', 'warm', 'medium', 'high', 'keep warm' etc. Few slow cookers come with continuous power variation mechanism. Other types of slow cookers don't have any temperature control settings and provide constant heat for several hours.

While cooking raw ingredients and a liquid of your choice (water, stock or wine etc) are arranged in the pot. For some recipes already warm liquid may be added. Then the lid is put on it and cooker is switched on.

Some cookers keep on cooking at same temperature and some may automatically switch from cooking mode to warming mode (71–74 °C / 160–165 °F). There is a probe inserted to measure the temperature which determines the switching point between different modes.

The heat of material inside the pot is maintained generally at temperature from 79–93 °C (175–200 °F) during cooking.
It can be adjusted according to the need of the recipe. Vapor produced from the heat inside the pot accumulates near the lid and turns into liquid and comes back. Some vitamins (water soluble) are filtered into the liquid. The lid helps prevent the vapor from escaping from the content while cooking and also while cooling. The liquid passes the heat from vessel wall to the raw ingredients and also spreads the flavor.

Some slow cookers need to be manually switched on and off, before and after cooking whereas others have automatic function for these activities.

The most efficient and latest slow cookers even have computerized control operations (e.g. you can program and set cooking for two hours on high, two hours on medium, two hours on low and then keep warm for another two hours and switch it off and also can set a timer to delay the start of cooking). That's what is called proper effortless cooking.

As the food cooked in the crock-pot remains warm in it for long, the effort in re-heating your prepared meal can be eliminated. You can also carry your crock-pot with you along with the prepared meal without the fear of the food spilling out of the pot as the lid of the cooker can be sealed fully.

As the slow cooker operates completely different, regular recipes should be modified a bit to cook in it. Liquid quantity should be manipulated according to the evaporation rate in slow cooker and also one should see that the container has enough liquid for the quantity of food. The dishes cooked in a slow cooker turn out to be really scrumptious.

1.3. Maintenance and care:

As with any other trusty appliance, a slow cooker needs special care and maintenance.

- → It can only be disassembled for cleaning by the user. For any repair work or anything else, disassembling should be done by experts. For servicing, always call professional appliance service men.
- → Abrupt temperature changes should be avoided. When the glass lid or the stoneware is hot, do not suddenly put them in cold water or keep them on any wet platform.
- → The container shouldn't be used for storing the food in refrigerator. If for some reason you have done that, then please remember not to re-heat it immediately after taking it out from refrigerator. Abrupt temperature changes may cause your stoneware to crack.
- → If you notice any crack on the stoneware or on the lid, then do not use it. It is no longer safe.
- → Keep it clean always.

Cleaning:

- → The base unit of the cooker and the plug should never be immersed in water. Keep them aside while cleaning.
- → Never forget to unplug the cooker from any electrical source and let it cool fully before starting the cleaning process.
- → You can clean the glass lid and the stoneware in the dishwasher. Keep the stoneware away from other utensils in the dishwasher to make sure it does not get damaged.
- → To remove leftover food or food stains from stoneware, fill it up with lukewarm soap water and leave it soak for 10-15 minutes. Take some baking soda on a plastic scouring pad

(Do not use steelwool or you will scratch your stoneware) and apply it on the surface of the cooker while cleaning.
→ Apply distilled white vinegar to wipe out any water stain or mineral accumulation inside the stoneware. If the stain is deep, apply a little vinegar, let it soak for few minutes, rinse it and then let it dry.
→ Take a damp, soft cloth to wipe both inside and outside of the base unit. Never use rough clothes or cleaners as the surface may get damaged.

1.4. Advantages:

There is no doubt that the slow cooker has a lot of advantages compared to other cooking appliances. Here are some benefits:

a) Slow cooking can soften the lean muscles and connective tissues of meat that is very useful part of making healthy and tasty stews. On other cooking processes, these muscles and tissues are removed because they toughen the meat while cooking. A slow cooker helps maintain the food's integrity in a dish to its maximum possible level.

b) With adequate liquids, there is little to no chance for your meal to get burnt while cooking for so long because of the low temperature setting and uniform heating process of a slow cooker.

c) The timer of the slow cooker is very useful. You can even set the timer to start the cooking process at your convenience. Suppose you are leaving for office at 7 am, but you want the slow cooker to start cooking at 9 am. You can actually set the timer accordingly and cook your dish according to your preferred time, so that when you come back from office you get a nice, hot meal ready for you.

d) The slow cooker is amazing in keeping the food warm in it for long hours even after the cooking process is finished.

e) Crock-pot makes one pot meal, which spares us from cleaning many pots and pans after cooking. Moreover, its design with detachable parts makes the cleaning and maintenance process simpler.

f) To a certain degree, the slow cooker is safer than stove tops and ovens because its temperature remains much lower during the whole process of cooking.

1.5. Disadvantages:

Does a slow cooker really have any disadvantages? We wonder, really. It sounds crazy, but it's true that it has a very few drawbacks like any other appliances.

a) Many vegetables lose their vitamins and trace nutrients during the cooking process. However, as slow cooker has relatively low temperature settings, it partially prevents good enzymes from getting denatured compared to other high temperature cooking processes. Using blanched or pre-cooked vegetables may help to keep the vitamins and nutrients intact in vegetables.

b) Foods cooked in slow cooker should not be allowed to cool below 70 °C (158 °F) as at this temperature harmful bacteria can grow inside the cooker and spoil the food. Few of these harmful bacteria may even produce spores and toxins which don't go away even after re-heating.

c) If you have ingredients to be added at the last stage of cooking, then again you have to wait for long hours to allow that ingredient to cook thoroughly as slow cooker takes long time to cook each and every ingredient. However, it is worth waiting, because the outcome will be so scrumptious.

1.6. Cooking Tips:

In this recipe book we will concentrate on meat based dishes that we can cook with a slow cooker. It is always good to get some tips and tricks before we actually start cooking. So, here are a handful of important points to remember while cooking meat based dishes.

a) **Browning helps:** In general it is not compulsory or needed to brown the meat before cooking. However, in most cases it is seen, that browning is worth making the effort. It gives the meat dish an extra rich flavor and better texture. And we should specially brown the ground meat before they go into the slow cooker. It prevents clumping of the meat and also prevents the gravy from becoming extra greasy.

b) **Spice Generously:** Slow cooked meat dishes get their charm from various spices. You can add whole spice like cinnamon sticks, caraway seeds, coriander seeds, bay leaves, peppercorns etc and also dried herbs like oregano, rosemary etc. So, encourage yourself to add lots of spices in your meat recipe while cooking it. Make sure you don't overdo them. Fresh herbs and fragrant leaves, also make the meat preparations much more vibrant, so be free to sprinkle fresh parsley, cilantro etc once slow cooking is done.

c) **Add less liquid:** Compared to oven or stovetop cooked meat dishes, slow cooked meat dishes need less liquid. Because, the slow cooking process generates lots of steam that can't escape and turns into liquid. Also various meat pieces excrete water while getting boiled. So, you have to add liquid very carefully to avoid watery meat dishes at the end of the slow cooking cycle. Otherwise you will extra effort to dry out the liquid in excess and make the gravy thick.

d) **High or low heat setting?** For tender cut meats you can use high heat setting and your dish will be cooked much sooner. Whereas, for tough cut meats, you should prefer low heat setting and longer hours of cooking.

e) **Keep crock-pot lid closed:** If you are at home and making the day meal in a slow cooker, then you may tend to peek at the food and stir it, while cooking process is not yet terminated. However, it would be better if you can control the urge of peeking frequently and from stirring the food in between. The reason why is because every time you open the lid, you slow down the cooking process by at least 10 – 15 minutes. So, the more you stir it, the longer the meat will take time to cook and will surely test your patience. You may also get delayed for serving the meal for your guests. We know, slow cooker needs very little or no attention or supervision during cooking. So, it's you who have to minimize the number of stirring, keep the lid closed and ultimately your meal will be ready on time.

So, now we know quite a bit about the slow cooker or the crock-pot and by now you might have become curious to know how the crock-pot dishes will be? If so, then stick to the book, because there are plenty of scrumptious meat recipes coming on your way in the next section. Get your slow cooker today, try the recipes at home and enjoy the outcome of the most popular cooking style of the era.

1. Slow Cooked Chicken Tikka Masala

Believed to be of Asian origin, Chicken Tikka Masala is a very popular non-vegetarian delicacy that is loved by people from every corner of the world. It is basically a spicy dish with combination of roasted chicken chunks and juicy rich gravy. While cooking this dish you have full freedom to experiment with the ingredients of the gravy. The gravy may contain all or few of these ingredients; tomato puree, cream or coconut cream, yogurt, coriander paste and various ground spices. The orange color of the gravy can be achieved either by adding food color or turmeric powder and tomato puree. One survey revealed that there are total 48 different Chicken Tikka Masala recipes cooked and served worldwide. Now with a great slow cooker handy you can be assured to achieve a really mouth watering version for this recipe.

Preparation Time: 8 hours 10 minutes

Serves: 4

Ingredients:

- Tomato (crushed, canned) = 1 can of 15 ounce (420 grams)
- Onion (medium, chopped) = 1
- Garlic Cloves (chopped) = 2
- Tomato paste = 2 tablespoons (37.5 grams)
- Garam Masala (Indian ground spice mix) = 2 teaspoons (4 grams)
- Chicken Thighs (boneless, skinless) = 8 (1 ½ pounds / 681 grams)
- English Cucumber (halved, thinly sliced) = ½
- Cilantro leaves (fresh) = ¼ Cup (28 grams)
- Lemon juice (fresh) = 1 tablespoon (10 ml)

- Basmati or any other long grain white rice = 1 Cup (optional) (180 grams)
- Heavy cream = ½ Cup (120 grams)
- Kosher salt = 1 teaspoon (5 grams)
- Black Pepper = ½ teaspoon (1 gram)

Let's Cook:

1. Take a 4 to 6 quart slow cooker. Arrange crushed tomato, onion, garlic, tomato paste, Garam Masala, kosher salt (3/4 teaspoon / 3.75 grams) and black pepper (1/4 teaspoon / 0.5 gram) at the bottom of it.
2. Now place the chicken thighs on a layer over this.
3. Close the lid, switch the cooker on and let it cook on low heat setting for 7 – 8 hours or on high heat setting for 3 – 4 hours.
4. Take a small bowl; Toss the sliced cucumber and cilantro leaves in it while adding the lemon juice, salt (1/4 teaspoon / 1.2 gram) and black pepper (1/4 teaspoon / 0.5 gram) slowly. You can prepare this mix beforehand and refrigerate it for 7 – 8 hours. This whole step is optional.
5. Cook the rice just 20 minutes prior to serving the dish. This is also optional.
6. Once chicken is done, open the lid of the cooker and stir in the cream.
7. Now serve Chicken Tikka Masala with rice and cucumber relish. You can also garnish the dish with fresh cilantro. This lends additional nice aroma to the already spicy and flavorful dish.

2. Chicken with Mushrooms and Bacon

This is a very simple, healthy yet elegant recipe that can be served when you are expecting guests at your place. You can use vegetarian or meat bacon along with the chicken. The dish has completely different flavor and temptation that you will come to know only once you taste this. It's a must try dish. Have this slow cooked Chicken with Mushrooms and Bacon, and enjoy your meal to the fullest.

Preparation Time: 7 – 8 hours

Serves: 6

Ingredients:

- Bacon (sliced, diced) = ½ pound (227 grams)
- Chicken (cut into pieces) = 4 to 6 pound (1800 – 2700 grams)
- Dry White Wine = ½ Cup (125 ml) or vermouth = ¼ Cup (65 ml) + water ¼ Cup (65 ml)
- Small white mushrooms = ½ pound (227 grams)
- Small White Onions (frozen, thawed) = 1 Cup (120 grams)
- Garlic Cloves (chopped) = 6
- Fresh Rosemary Sprigs = 3 or dried rosemary leaves = 1 tablespoon (1.7 grams)
- Kosher Salt = 1 teaspoon (5 grams)
- Water = ¼ Cup (65 ml)
- Cornstarch = 2 tablespoons (16 grams)
- Broccoli florets (medium, cooked) = 1 Cup (85 grams) (optional)

Let's Cook:

1. First cook the bacon in a large skillet until they become crispy. Once done, transfer these to a 4 to 6 quart slow cooker with a slotted spoon.
2. Discard if there is any fat portion left on the skillet. Now in this skillet brown the meat over medium-high heat. Transfer the chicken after browning to the slow cooker as well.
3. Now pour the wine onto the skillet and scrape away any leftover portion of browned meat and add this to the slow cooker.
4. Now add the mushrooms, garlic, onion, salt and rosemary leaves or sprigs to the cooker.
5. Close the lid, switch the cooker on and let it cook on low heat setting for around 6 hours or on high heat setting for around 3 hours.
6. Transfer chicken, bacon and vegetables from the slow cooker to a platter and keep this warm. Now pour the remaining gravy out of the slow cooker onto a saucepan. Combine this with water and cornstarch.
7. Heat the mixture over medium-high flame and bring it to boil. Stir continuously, till the sauce thickens. Pour this sauce over the chicken on the platter and serve hot along with cooked broccoli.

3. Soy Braised Chicken

Before you decide to cook soy braised chicken, make sure you make it in good quantity to save yourself from regretting later. Because the dish will be so much adorable, scrumptious and tempting, you won't be able to control yourself from having it more than you thought or planned to. And same will be the case for your family members or friends or whoever will have it. You will get to know its temptation once you make this at home. So, what are you waiting for? Get the recipe, cook it and have a blast at meal time.

Preparation Time: 8 hours 10 minutes

Serves: 4

Ingredients:

- Onion (medium, sliced) = 2
- Garlic Cloves (smashed) = 4
- Apple Cider Vinegar = 1/3 Cup (85 ml)
- Soy Sauce = 1/3 Cup (85 grams)
- Brown sugar = 1 tablespoon (10 grams)
- Bay leaf = 1
- Chicken Thighs (skinless, bone-in) = 8 (1 ¾ pounds / 795 grams)
- Paprika = 1 teaspoon (2 grams)
- Long-grain white rice = 1 Cup (180 grams)
- Large head bok choy (cut into 1 inch strips) = 1
- Scallions (thinly sliced) = 2
- Black Pepper

Let's Cook:

1. Take a 5 – 6 quart slow cooker; Arrange onions, garlic, soy sauce, vinegar, brown sugar, bay leaf and black pepper (1/4 teaspoon / 0.5 grams) at the bottom of this.
2. Then layer the chicken thighs on this.
3. Close the lid, switch the cooker on and let it cook on low heat setting for 7 – 8 hours or on high heat setting 3 – 4 hours.
4. Cook the rice (according to the cooking instructions mentioned on its package) just 20 minutes prior to serving.
5. Turn the cooker to high heat setting (if it was running on low setting till now) for last 10 minutes of cooking. Open the lid, gently fold the bok choy into the chicken, cover and let it cook. It should become tender at the end of the cooking cycle.
6. Now the soy braised, glazy chicken is ready to serve.
7. Have it and relish the joy of your taste buds.

4. Jalapeno chicken

Chicken dishes are always very special and interesting. However, they can be more interesting when combined with jalapeno. Jalapeno chicken has a unique flavor that can win your heart over and can give your meal a nice twist. Here is such a Jalapeno chicken recipe that you can cook with slow cooker effortlessly and make your weekend meal a special one. Here is the recipe coming your way.

Preparation Time: 5 – 6 hours

Serves: 6

Ingredients:

- Chicken breasts (skinless, bone-in, halved) = 6
- Chili Powder = 1 tablespoon (7.5 grams)
- Low-sodium chicken broth = ½ Cup (125 ml)
- Lemon juice = 2 tablespoons (30 ml)
- Jalapeno Chile Pepper (sliced, pickled, drained) = 1/3 Cup
- Cornstarch = 1 tablespoon (8 grams)
- Low-fat cream cheese (softened, cut into cubes) – 1 package of 8 ounce (22 grams)
- Regular Bacon or Turkey Bacon (cooked to crispy, drained, crumbled) = 2 slices (optional)
- Cold water = 1 tablespoon (15 ml)
- Salt = 1/8 teaspoon (0.6 grams)

Let's Cook:

1. First sprinkle some chili powder and salt on the chicken pieces and rub the surface.
2. Take a 4 to 6 quart slow cooker; Place chicken (bone side down) in this and pour in the broth and lemon juice on it. Top it with Jalapeno Chile pepper.
3. Close the lid, switch the cooker on and let it cook on low heat setting for 5 – 6 hours or on high heat setting for 2 ½ - 3 hours.
4. Open the lid, transfer chicken and jalapeno to a platter leaving the liquid back in the cooker. Cover the chicken in the platter to keep warm.
5. Take a small bowl, mix the cornstarch with water and stir in to the liquid in the cooker. If the cooker was running on low heat setting, now turn it to high. Add the cream cheese and whisk to combine well. Close the lid again and let it cook for another 15 minutes or until the gravy thickens.
6. Pour this sauce over the chicken in the platter and sprinkle the bacon on it.
7. Jalapeno chicken is absolutely ready to be served and eaten. Enjoy it.

5. Angel Chicken

This is another chicken dish accompanied by an Italian, thin, hair-like pasta called Angel pasta. The fine texture and smoothness of this pasta is the specialty of this dish. The combination of this pasta with chicken, vegetables and spices makes this a really special one and you would be overwhelmed by having such a marvelous chicken preparation. Check out the recipe and plan to make this over next weekend. Your weekend meal will be a super hit one with this wonderful dish.

Preparation Time: 4 – 5 hours

Serves: 4

Ingredients:

- Chicken breasts (skinless, boneless, halved) =4 (about 1 ½ pounds / 681 grams)
- Vegetable oil = 1 tablespoon (optional) (14 grams)
- Fresh button Mushrooms (quartered) = 1 package of 8 ounce (224 grams)
- Fresh Shiitake Mushrooms (caps sliced, stems removed) = 1 package of 8 ounce (224 grams)
- Butter = ¼ Cup (60 grams)
- Italian dry salad dressing mix = 1 package of 0.7 ounce (20 grams)
- Condensed Golden Mushroom Soup = 1 can of 10 ¾ ounce (320 ml)
- Dry White Wine = ½ Cup (125 ml)
- Cream cheese spread with onion and chives = ½ of a 8 ounce tub (112 grams)
- Angel hair pasta (cooked)

- Green onion (sliced) or fresh chives (snipped) – (optional)

Let's Cook:

1. Put the vegetable oil on a large skillet over medium-high heat and brown the chicken before putting into the slow cooker.
2. Take a 3 ½ or 4 quart slow cooker, arrange all the mushrooms at the bottom of it and top with the browned chicken.
3. Heat a medium saucepan over low-medium flame, melt the butter in it and stir in Italian salad dressing mix with a slotted spoon. Add in mushroom soup, white wine and cream cheese. Keep stirring until all are combined together. Pour this over the chicken in the slow cooker.
4. Close the lid, switch the cooker on and let it cook on low heat setting for 4 – 5 hours.
5. Serve the chicken along with the cooked Angel pasta in a plate. Sprinkle chives if you wish.

6. Chicken, Shrimp Jambalaya

It is something similar to Paella of Spain. Both of which have combination of chicken, seafood, rice, varieties of vegetables and spices. Jambalaya has many varieties according to the combination of ingredients and all of them are equally, blissfully tasty. Here is a variety of this mouthwatering dish that you will love for sure. The Cajun seasoning lends it an extra flavor and lots of lean proteins make the dish a healthy one. Let's get the detailed recipe and try it.

Preparation Time: 5 – 6 hours

Serves: 8

Ingredients:

- Chicken breasts or thighs (skinless, boneless, halved and then cut into ¾' pieces) = 1 ½ pounds (681 grams)
- Celery (thinly sliced) = 2 Cups (250 grams)
- Tomatoes (unsalted, diced, undrained) = 1 can of 14 ½ ounce (405 grams)
- Low-sodium chicken broth = 1 can of 14 ounce (420 ml)
- Tomato paste (unsalted) = 1/3 Cup (75 grams) or ½ can of 6 ounce (84 grams)
- Unsalted Cajun seasoning = 1 ½ tablespoons (6.5 grams)
- Garlic Cloves (minced) = 2
- Instant brown rice (uncooked) = 1 ⅓ Cups (295 grams)
- Red, green or yellow sweet pepper = ¾ Cup (130 grams)
- Shrimp (fresh or frozen, peeled, deveined, cooked) = 12 ounces (336 grams)
- Italian parsley (flat leaf, snipped) = 2 tablespoons (2 grams)
- Celery leaves (optional)

- Salt = ½ teaspoon (2.5 grams)

Let's Cook:

1. Take a 4 quart slow cooker; Arrange chicken, onion, celery, tomatoes (with juice), tomato paste, garlic, salt and Cajun seasoning in this.
2. Close the lid, switch the cooker on and let it cook on low heat setting for 4 ½ – 5 ½ hours or on high heat setting for 2 ¼ - 2 ¾ hours.
3. Turn the cooker heat setting to high (if it was running on low heat setting till now, otherwise keep it on high only), stir in the uncooked brown rice, sweet pepper and let it cook for another half an hour or until the rice is tender and all the liquid is absorbed.
4. Now thaw shrimp (if frozen), stir in to the chicken in the slow cooker. Also add in the parsley.
5. The Jambalaya is ready to be served. If you wish garnish with celery leaves.

7. Coq Au Vin

French cuisine will always surprise you with its delectable dishes. Coq Au Vin comes from there and is superbly flavorful and tastes truly divine. It has wine braised chicken and lots of veggies to accompany the chicken and to enhance the richness. The name 'Coq Au Vin' suggests 'rooster/cock braised with wine'. Traditionally burgundy wine is used, however, there are many versions that use any local wine and the outcome is always awesome. It's simple enough to cook at home. Just get a slow cooker and follow the recipe.

Preparation Time: 5 – 6 hours

Serves: 4

Ingredients:

- Chicken Thighs (skinless) = 3 pounds (1.3 kg)
- Envelope beef onion soup mix = ½ of a 2.2 ounce package (30 grams)
- Fresh Mushrooms (quartered) = 2 Cups (150 grams)
- Small whole onions (frozen) = 1 ½ Cups (150 grams)
- Carrots (medium, cut into 3 ½ inch slices) = 3
- Dry red wine = ½ Cup (125 ml)
- Mashed potatoes (hot, cooked, optional)
- Fresh parsley (snipped, optional)
- Non stick cooking spray

Let's Cook:

1. Take a large skillet, coat it lightly with non stick cooking spray and now heat it over medium flame. Brown the chicken thighs in this and drain off the fat portion.
2. Take a 3 ½ or 4 quart slow cooker; arrange the chicken at the bottom of this. Sprinkle the dry onion soup mix on this.
3. Now add mushrooms, carrots and onion. Pour the red wine all over the other ingredients in the slow cooker.
4. Close the lid, switch the cooker on and let it cook on low heat setting for 5 – 6 hours or on high heat setting for 2 ½ - 3 hours.
5. Open the lid and a nice aroma will fill the air around you.
6. If you wish serve the dish with mashed potatoes and sprinkle with parsley.

8. Sweet, sour and saucy chicken

Another chicken recipe from Asian cuisine awaits you here. It has completely different taste and flavor. It goes well with white rice and believed to have soothing effect in summer season. However, it can be relished in any season and at any time. Try it once and you will be lost in its magnificent sweet and sour taste. The recipe is here for you to look at.

Preparation Time: 6 – 7 hours

Serves: 4 - 6

Ingredients:

- Chicken thighs or breast halves or drumsticks (skinless, boneless) = 2 ½ - 3 pounds (1.1 kg – 1.3 kg)
- Lemonade concentrate (frozen, thawed) = ½ of a 12 ounce can (180 ml) or about ¾ Cup (185 ml)
- Brown sugar = 3 tablespoons (30 grams)
- Ketchup = 3 tablespoons (42 grams)
- Vinegar = 1 tablespoon (13 grams)
- Cornstarch = 2 tablespoons (16 grams)
- Cold water = 2 tablespoons (28 ml)
- Salt = ¼ teaspoon (1.2 grams)
- Fried rice or hot cooked white rice

Let's Cook:

1. It would be good if you can use a 3 ½ or 4 quart slow cooker. Arrange the chicken pieces at the bottom of this. Sprinkle some salt.
2. Take a medium bowl; put the lemonade concentrate, ketchup, brown sugar and vinegar. Mix well. Pour this over the chicken pieces in the slow cooker.
3. Close the lid, switch the cooker on and let it cook on low heat setting for 6 – 7 hours or on high heat setting for 3 – 3 ½ hours.
4. Transfer the chicken with a slotted spoon to a platter leaving the liquid back in the cooker. Cover the platter in order to keep the chicken warm.
5. Take a medium sauce pan and pour the left over liquid from the cooker onto this. Discard the fat portion, if there is any. Mix cornstarch with cold water. Pour this into the liquid in sauce pan. Heat this over medium flame and keep stirring until the sauce thickens. Stir and keep cooking for another couple of minutes.
6. Pour this sauce evenly on the chicken.
7. Now the sweet, sour and saucy chicken is ready. Serve it with hot cooked white rice.

9. Cranberry Chicken

Are you ready to try some very different chicken dish? How about a cranberry flavored one? "It would be divine" I must say. We know cranberry is so versatile that it can be used in many dishes in many ways and also it can be great as part of a healthy diet. It helps in getting over Urinary tract infections, cardiovascular disease, even cancer and also improves dental health. You can have it raw, as juice, can add in salad, combine with hard drinks and yes, also can add it as sauce in chicken preparation! If it sounds great to you, then try this cranberry chicken today and trust me, you won't regret.

Preparation Time: 5 – 6 hours

Serves: 6

Ingredients:

- Chicken Thighs or drumsticks (skinless) = 2 ½ - 3 pounds (1.1 kg – 1.3 kg)
- Whole Cranberry sauce = 1 can of 16 ounce (450 grams)
- Dry onion soup mix = 2 tablespoons (12 grams)
- Quick-cooking Tapioca = 2 tablespoons (20 grams)
- Hot cooked rice = 3 Cups (540 grams) (optional)
- Broccoli (for serving, optional)

Let's Cook:

1. Take a 3 ½ or 4 quart slow cooker. Arrange chicken pieces in this. Pour in the cranberry sauce onto it. Also add dry onion soup mix and Tapioca. Combine all nicely.

2. Close the lid, switch the cooker on and let it cook on low heat setting for 5 – 6 hours or on high heat setting for 2 ½ - 3 hours.
3. Cranberry chicken is ready. Serve it with hot rice and/or broccoli or whatever you wish. It will taste awesome in any way.

10. Cashew Chicken

Cashew chicken is a super tasty lean meat dish. The combination of stir fried and slow cooked chicken with roasted cashews seems to be just heavenly and unimaginably tempting. Try out this savory dish whenever you have a party at home and surprise your guests with this superb Chinese delicacy. It can be served with cooked rice or bread or salad or just a glass of wine. It goes well with any combination. The process of making this dish is very easy and so anyone can make this. The detailed recipe is here for you.

Preparation Time: 6 – 8 hours

Serves: 6

Ingredients:

- Golden Mushroom Soup (condensed) = 1 can of 10 ¾ ounce (322 ml)
- Soy sauce = 3 tablespoons (48 grams)
- Ginger (ground) = 1 teaspoon (1.8 grams)
- Chicken Tenders = 1 ½ pounds (681 grams)
- Broccoli (frozen) or stir fried vegetable mix = 1 package of 16 ounce (450 grams)
- Mushrooms (sliced, drained) = 1 can of 4 ounce (112 grams)
- Cashews = ½ Cup (75 grams)
- Cooked brown rice (optional)

Let's Cook:

1. Take a 3 ½ or 4 quart slow cooker. Add ginger, soy sauce and mushroom soup in this. Then stir in the chicken, broccoli or stir-fried vegetables and mushrooms. Mix well.

2. Close the lid, switch the cooker on and let it cook on low temperature setting for 6 – 8 hours or on high setting for 3 - 4 hours.
3. Open the lid, stir in the cashews now and spoon out the chicken on a serving plate.
4. If you wish serve with hot cooked rice, otherwise just have it like that.

11. Chicken Cacciatore

The word "cacciatore' means 'hunter'. So, the dish can be called as 'hunter-style' chicken. It brings its essence from Italian cuisine, the favorite for all. It has many versions and styles for cooking. The sauce or gravy used in this can be of many types and flavors. The chicken is braised in this dish and so lends extra richness to the whole thing. Once you cook with your slow cooker and taste it, you will add this to your list of favorite dishes for sure. For now, let's peek at the recipe.

Preparation Time: 6 – 7 hours

Serves: 6

Ingredients:

- All purpose flour = 3 Cups (390 grams)
- Chicken breasts or thighs or drumsticks (halved, skinned) = 3 ½ - 4 pounds (1.5 kg – 1.8 kg)
- Olive oil = 2 tablespoons (28 grams)
- Button or Cremini mushrooms (thinly sliced) = 2 Cups (150 grams)
- Tomatoes (diced, drained) = 1 can of 14 ½ ounce (406 grams)
- Green Sweet Pepper (chopped) = 1 large
- Onion (chopped) = 1 large
- Carrots (chopped) = 2 medium
- Dry White wine = ½ Cup (125 ml)
- Fresh Basil (snipped) = 2 tablespoons (5.3 grams)
- Fresh Italian Parsley (flat leaf) = 2 tablespoons (3 grams)

- Fresh Thyme leaves = 1 teaspoon (1.43 grams)
- Black Pepper (ground) = ½ teaspoon (1 gram)
- Salt = ½ teaspoon (2.5 grams)

Let's Cook:

1. Put the all purpose flour in a plastic bag. Add the chicken pieces (a few at a time) and shake the bag to coat the chicken pieces with flour. Coat all the chicken pieces like this.
2. Now take a large skillet, heat olive oil in this over medium-high flame and add the chicken pieces. Let the chicken pieces get browned. It will take about 10 -12 minutes. Flip the chicken pieces on both sides in between to make sure they get browned all over.
3. Transfer the browned chicken pieces to a 5 or 6 quart slow cooker.
4. Now in the same skillet, add mushrooms and cook by stirring for 2 – 3 minutes. Transfer the stir fried mushrooms to the slow cooker.
5. Now add drained tomatoes, onion, green sweet pepper, carrots, white wine, salt and black pepper to the mixture of chicken and mushroom in the slow cooker.
6. Close the lid, switch the cooker on and let it cook on low heat setting for 6 – 7 hours or on high heat setting for 3 – 3 ½ hours.
7. Once done, stir in the basil, thyme leaves and Italian parsley to the chicken and serve.

12. Chicken Sloppy Joe

Sloppy Joe is an American sandwich that is eaten in main course. It is a very quick and easy meal. And you must make it if you have little ones in your home. They will absolutely love it. The dish can be versatile. This particular sloppy Joe has chicken / turkey – pork filling that you can put into toasted or flour tortilla and make different types of meals as per your choice. Let's look at the recipe now.

Preparation Time: 6 – 8 hours

Serves: 16 - 20

Ingredients:

- Chicken or Turkey (ground, uncooked) = 1 ½ pounds (681 grams)
- Pork (ground) = 1 ½ pounds (681 grams)
- Onion (chopped) = 2 large
- Salsa (medium hot, bottled) = 4 Cups (968 grams)
- Green Sweet Pepper (chopped) = 2 medium
- Whole Kernel Corn (fresh or frozen) = 1 ½ Cups (262 grams)
- Chipotle pepper in Adobo sauce (canned, chopped) = 2 tablespoons (28 grams)
- Chili Powder = 1 tablespoon (7.5 grams)
- Coriander (ground) = 1 ½ teaspoons (1 gram)
- Hoagie Rolls or Flour tortilla (6 inch, split, toasted) = 16 – 20
- Vegetable oil (as needed)
- Garlic salt = 1 ½ teaspoons (7 grams)

For Topping (optional)

- Cilantro (chopped)
- Tomato (chopped)
- Avocado (diced)
- Cotija cheese (crumbled)

Let's Cook:

1. Take a large skillet; Put ground chicken / turkey, ground pork, onions and cook until meats get browned nicely. Onions should be tender. Keep crumbling the meats with a wooden spoon while cooking.
2. Once done, transfer the meat and onion to a 4 or 5 quart slow cooker. Discard the fat portion, if any.
3. Add sweet pepper, salsa, kernel corn, chipotle pepper, coriander, chili powder and garlic salt in the slow cooker. Mix with meat mixture nicely.
4. Close the lid, switch the cooker on and let it cook on low heat setting for 6 – 8 hours or on high heat setting for 3 - 4 hours.
5. Meanwhile you can keep the tortillas ready by toasting them in hot oil for 2 – 3 minutes. Remove them from oil using tongs and fold them over wire rack lined with paper towel. Let them cool until little firm.
6. Once the slow cooker cycle is over, spoon the meat filling out from the cooker onto each tortilla, add toppings of your choice and serve.

13. Cheesy Chicken with Penne Pasta

Who doesn't love cheesy chicken? Everybody does. And when the yummy chicken is accompanied with penne pasta it becomes more luscious. It's a special treat from Italian cuisine that you can make at any time and your meal will be a fun meal. While cooking this dish in slow cooker your kitchen will be filled with nice tempting aroma that will blow your mind away. The recipe of this yummy chicken is here. Get it now.

Preparation Time: 5 – 6 hours

Serves: 4

Ingredients:

- Egg = 1
- Plain Bread Crumbs (preferably Progresso) = 1/3 Cup (43 grams)
- Italian seasoning = ½ teaspoon (0.7 grams)
- Parmesan cheese (shredded) = 1/3 Cup (80 grams)
- Chicken breasts (halved, skinless, boneless) = 4
- Tomato pasta sauce = 1 jar of 26 oz (728 grams)
- Italian Cheese blend (shredded) = ½ Cup (2 oz / 56 grams)
- Penne Pasta (uncooked) = 2 2/3 Cups (8 oz / 224 grams)
- Salt = ¼ teaspoon (1.2 grams)
- Black Pepper = ¼ teaspoon (0.5 gram)
- Non stick cooking spray

Let's Cook:

1. Apply non stick cooking spray to a 2 or 3 quart slow cooker.
2. Take a small shallow bowl; Beat the egg in this.

3. In a separate shallow bowl, mix bread crumbs, Italian seasoning, parmesan cheese, black pepper and salt.
4. Dip the chicken pieces into the beaten egg, and then coat them with bread crumb mixture. Place the coated chicken pieces in the slow cooker.
5. Close the lid, switch the cooker on and let it cook on low heat setting for 5 – 6 hours.
6. Once done, sprinkle the Italian cheese blend over the chicken.
7. Again close the lid and let it cook for another 10 minutes on low heat setting. The cheese blend should melt and cover the chicken pieces nicely.
8. Cook the penne pasta as per package instructions and keep aside meanwhile.
9. Once the chicken is cooked, serve it with the pasta and enjoy your meal.

14. Italian tangy chicken with Artichokes

It's another Italian chicken dish with tangy flavor of tomatoes and goodness of nutritious artichokes. Artichoke is visually fascinating as well as delightful as food. It is low in calorie, rich in nutrients and also a good source of vitamins. Get fresh artichokes from market and prepare this ambrosial dish. Recipe is right here for you.

Preparation Time: 4 – 5 hours

Serves: 4

Ingredients:

- Chicken Breasts (bone-in) = 4 (2 ½ pounds / 1.1 kg)
- Italian Vinaigrette dressing or fat free Balsamic dressing = 3 tablespoons (50 grams)
- Italian seasoning = 1 teaspoon (1.5 grams)
- Onion (thinly sliced) = 1 Cup (120 grams)
- Green Olives (sliced) = ¼ Cup (45 grams)
- Garlic Cloves (finely chopped) = 4
- Tomatoes (diced, drained) = 1 can of 14.5 oz (406 grams)
- Artichokes (quartered, drained) = 1 can of 14 oz (392 grams)
- Fresh parsley (finely chopped) = 2 – 3 tablespoons (3 – 4.5 grams)
- Salt = ½ teaspoon (2.5 grams)
- Black Pepper = ¼ teaspoon (0.5 gram)
- Non stick cooking spray

Let's Cook:

1. Take a 3 or 4 quart slow cooker and apply the no stick cooking spray lightly to coat evenly.

2. Remove the skin and any fat portion present in the chicken pieces. Brush the chicken pieces with the dressings and place them in the cooker.
3. Sprinkle Italian seasoning, pepper and salt on the chicken pieces.
4. Add all the remaining ingredients except the parsley.
5. Close the lid, switch the cooker on and let it cook on low heat setting for 4 ½ – 5 ½ hours.
6. Drain off any fat that surfaced on the chicken mixture. Now the dish is ready.
7. Sprinkle the parsley and serve in a shallow serving bowl.

15. Chicken Noodles Alfredo

Here is another chicken delicacy which is rich, creamy and full of veggies, noodles apart from chicken. The combination of chicken and noodles is magnificent and it fascinates everyone. Slow cooking gives this dish an extra flavor and smoothness that you will just die for. Like any other slow cooker recipe this one is also a super easy one to make at home. You can add any vegetables of your choice in this. So, try this for sure. The full recipe is jotted down below.

Preparation Time: 6 – 7 hours

Serves: 5

Ingredients:

- Chicken Thighs (skinless, boneless, cut into ¾ inch pieces) = 1 pound (454 grams)
- Artichokes (quartered, drained) = 1 can of 14 oz (392 grams)
- Alfredo pasta sauce = 1 jar of 16 oz (448 grams)
- Water = 1 Cup (235 ml)
- Sun-dried tomatoes (chopped) = ½ Cup (27 grams)
- Medium egg noodles (uncooked) = 3 Cups (225 grams)
- Parmesan cheese (shredded) = 2 tablespoons (30 grams)

Let's Cook:

1. Take a 3 or 4 quart slow cooker. Combine chicken pieces, artichokes, pasta sauce and water in this.
2. Close the lid, switch the cooker on and let it cook on low heat setting for 5 – 6 hours.
3. Stir in the tomatoes and uncooked noodles to the chicken mixture in the cooker just 25 minutes prior to serving. Turn

the heat setting of the cooker to high and let it cook again for about 15 – 20 minutes or until the noodles are tender.
4. Ladle the chicken to the serving bowls, sprinkle shredded parmesan cheese over every bowl of chicken and serve hot.

16. Spiced slow-cooked Beef Sloppy Joes

One can't get bored of having sloppy Joes. They are so crispy, spicy yet very much filling. Beef sloppy Joes can give you so satisfying meal that can keep your tummy happy and also keep you going for long. It is rich, spicy and has tingling taste which will be good treat for your taste buds. Go through the recipe and try this at home for dinner tonight. Have fun having this spicy beef sloppy Joes.

Preparation Time: 7 – 8 hours

Serves: 6

Ingredients:

- Lean beef (ground) = 2 pounds (908 grams)
- Salsa = 2 jars of 16 ounce each (total 896 grams)
- Fresh mushrooms (sliced) = 3 Cups (225 grams)
- Carrots (shredded) = 3 medium (1 ½ Cup / 135 grams)
- Green and/or Red sweet pepper (finely chopped) = 1 ½ Cups (262 grams)
- Tomato paste = 1/3 Cup (100 grams)
- Basil (dried, crushed) = 2 teaspoons (2.8 grams)
- Oregano (dried, crushed) = 2 teaspoons (3.6 grams)
- Cayenne Pepper = ¼ teaspoon (0.5 gram)
- Garlic cloves (minced) = 4
- Salt – ½ teaspoon (2.5 grams)
- Kaiser Rolls (split, toasted) = 6

Let's Cook:

1. Take a large skillet, brown the beef in it nicely till aroma comes out of it. Keep stirring in between with slotted spoon

and break the meat into tiny pieces. Once done, drain off the fat and transfer the beef to a 5-6 quart slow cooker.
2. Add carrots, mushrooms, salsa, sweet pepper, basil, tomato paste, oregano, garlic, cayenne pepper and salt in the slow cooker. Mix all together nicely with a spoon.
3. Close the lid, switch the cooker on and let it cook on low heat for 8 – 10 hours or on high heat for 4 - 5 hours.
4. Once done, scoop out the beef mixture from the cooker and place on the toasted Kaiser rolls and serve.
5. If any extra beef mixture is left over, you can keep this covered, refrigerate and have it later as Taco salad.

17. Beer Braised Beef Ribs

Making beer braised beef ribs is more of a fun than a cooking process. It incorporates a very few ingredients and you will be amazed to see how a simple process with these ingredients can end up in such a fabulous treat. When you slow cook vegetables, they tend to release their sugar content in the long cooking process. And the beer, after spending significant time in slow cooker releases fat and lends richness to the dish. The beauty of this particular dish is that you can be flexible with the ingredients and can use different meats and vegetables. So, get ready to cook this tempting dish and have fun.

Preparation Time: 11 – 12 hours

Serves: 4 - 6

Ingredients:

- Beef Short Ribs = 5 pounds (2.3 kg)
- Beef broth = 1 can of 14 ounce (420 ml)
- Dark Beer (any brand of your choice) = 1 can of 12 ounce (360 ml)
- Onion (medium, cut into thin wedges) = 1
- Molasses = ¼ Cup (80 grams)
- Balsamic Vinegar = 2 tablespoons (26 grams)
- Thyme (dried, crushed) = 1 teaspoon (1.43 grams)
- Hot pepper sauce (bottled) = 1 teaspoon (5.3 grams)
- Mashed potatoes / hot buttered noodles (optional)
- Fresh thyme leaves (optional)
- Salt = ½ teaspoon (2.5 grams)

Let's Cook:

1. Place the beef short ribs in a 5 or 6 quart slow cooker. Add in beef broth, dark beer, onion, vinegar, molasses, thyme, salt, and hot pepper sauce to the beef ribs in the cooker. Mix well.
2. Close the lid, switch the cooker on and let it cook on low heat setting for 11 – 12 hours or on high heat setting for 5 ½ - 6 hours.
3. Once done, open the lid, take out the beef ribs with a slotted spoon and keep in a platter. Cover this to keep the cooked beef ribs warm. Drain off the fat from the liquid left in the cooker. Now add the liquid to the beef.
4. Garnish with thyme leaves and you can just have it like this or else serve with mashed potatoes. The beer braised ribs will taste divine in any way.

18. Slow cooked Beef Goulash

Here is a Hungarian Beef preparation that is spicy yet very satisfying. It has complete combo of meat, lots of veggies, flavor of paprika and other spices. You can adjust the spice levels. If your taste buds are flexible enough to taste foods from different continents, then it would be a great idea to have Beef Goulash for a meal. Once you have this, you will suggest your friends to taste this as well for sure. Yeah, this is truly such a mouth watering dish. The recipe is here:

Preparation Time: 8 – 9 hours

Serves: 6

Ingredients:

- Beef stew meat = 1 ½ pounds (681 grams)
- Carrots (medium, cut in bias into ½ inch sticks) = 2
- Onion (medium, thinly sliced) = 2
- Garlic Cloves (minced) = 3
- Beef Broth = 1 ¼ Cups (315 ml)
- Tomato Paste = 1 can of 6 ounce (168 grams)
- Hungarian Paprika = 1 tablespoon (7 grams)
- Lemon peel (finely shredded) = 1 teaspoon (5 grams)
- Caraway Seeds = ½ teaspoon (1 gram)
- Bay leaf = 1
- Green or red sweet peppers (cut into bite size pieces) = 1
- Salt = ½ teaspoon (2.5 grams)
- Black Pepper (ground) = ¼ teaspoon (0.5 gram)
- Noodles (hot cooked) (as needed)
- Yoghurt or dairy sour cream (as needed)

Let's Cook:

1. Take a 3 ½ or 4 quart slow cooker. Arrange beef, onions, garlic and carrots in this.
2. Take a small bowl; Mix beef broth, paprika, tomato paste, caraway seeds, lemon peel, black pepper, salt and bay leaf in this. Pour this mixture into the slow cooker.
3. Close the lid, switch the cooker on and let it cook on low heat for 8 – 9 hours or on high heat for 3 ½ - 4 ½ hours.
4. Turn the slow cooker heat setting to high (if it was running on low till now), stir in the sweet pepper and close the lid. Let it again cook for about 30 more minutes. Remove and discard the bay leaf.
5. Top the beef Goulash with Yoghurt or dairy sour cream and sprinkle some more paprika if you wish.
6. Serve this hot with cooked noodles or as it is.

19. Slow Cooked Beef Lo Mein

Another beef delicacy and this time it is from Asian cuisine. Homemade slow cooked version of beef lo Mein tastes fabulous. If you are health and calorie conscious, you can use more of vegetables and less of oil. The outcome will still be much adorable and will deserve much appreciation. The readymade sauce makes your job even easier. Overall this is a super tasty and super easy dish that you can make effortlessly at home any time. Let's go through the recipe now.

Preparation Time: 7 – 9 hours

Serves: 8

Ingredients:

- Beef Sirloin steak (boneless, cut into 1 inch thick pieces) = 2 pounds (908 grams)
- Cooking oil = 1 tablespoon (14 grams)
- Onion (large, sliced) = 1
- Water chestnuts (sliced, drained) = 1 can of 8 ounce (224 grams)
- Whole Mushrooms (drained) = 1 jar of 4 ½ ounce (128 grams)
- Stir-fry sauce = 1 jar of 12 ounce (336 grams)
- Quick cooking Tapioca = 1 tablespoon (9.5 grams)
- Broccoli, carrots and cauliflower (frozen, loosely packed) = 1 package of 16 ounce (450 grams)
- Cashews = 1/3 Cup (50 grams)
- Lo Mein noodles (dried) = 12 ounces (336 grams)

Let's Cook:

1. Trim off fat portion from the meat. Take a large skillet and brown the meat in two batches in hot cooking oil. Again drain off extra fat from meat. Keep it aside.
2. Take a 3 ½ or 4 quart slow cooker; arrange the browned meat, mushrooms and water chestnuts.
3. In another small bowl combine tapioca and stir-fry sauce. Pour this onto the mixture in the cooker.
4. Close the lid, switch the cooker on and let it cook on low heat setting for 7 – 9 hours or on high heat setting for 3 ½ - 4 ½ hours.
5. Turn the slow cooker heat setting to high (if it was running on low till now), stir in all the frozen vegetables and again cover it. Let it cook for about 30 – 40 minutes more or until all vegetables are done or have become crispy.
6. Now stir in the cashews.
7. Meanwhile, cook the Lo Mein noodles according to its package instructions, drain and keep aside.
8. Once the beef is cooked, mix this with the cooked Lo Mein noodles nicely and serve.

20. Corned Beef with Orange-spice

Corned beef might be a common recipe, however when you add molasses, dry fruits, orange juice, tapioca etc and prefer a slow cooking process to make this, it becomes a very special one, rather the best corned beef dish indeed. The regular corned beef will liven up to be an aromatic, spicy and tempting one. And as slow cooker makes any cooking process simpler and effortless, making this dish becomes more of a fun. So, get the recipe and get ready to make this awesomely tasty corned beef.

Preparation Time: 8 – 10 hours

Serves: 6

Ingredients:

- Corned Beef Brisket = 2 ½ - 3 pounds (1.1 – 1.3 kg)
- Mixed dried fruit = 1 package of 7 ounce (196 grams)
- Dried Cranberries = ½ Cup (50 grams)
- Quick Cooking Tapioca = 2 tablespoons (20 grams)
- Orange Juice = ½ Cup (125 ml)
- Water = ½ Cup (118 ml)
- Molasses (mild flavored) = 1 tablespoon (20 grams)
- Cinnamon (ground) = ¼ teaspoon (0.5 gram)
- Nutmeg (ground) = 1/8 teaspoon (0.3 gram)

Let's Cook.

1. Trim off the fat portion from the meat. If needed, cut it into small pieces for trimming the fat off. Transfer all the meats to a 3 ½ or 4 quart slow cooker.

2. If any of those dried fruits came large pieces, cut them into smaller ones. Sprinkle the dried fruits, tapioca and dried cranberries over the meat in the slow cooker.
3. Take a small bowl; Mix water, orange juice, cinnamon powder, molasses and nutmeg powder in this. Pour this mixture over the meat mixture in the slow cooker.
4. Close the lid, switch the cooker on and let it cook on low heat setting for 8 – 10 hours or on high heat setting for 4 - 5 hours.
5. Once done, remove the meat from the cooker with a slotted spoon and put on a plate. Cut the meat into thin slices grain wise. Transfer and arrange the meat pieces on a serving platter. Pour the fruit mixture from the cooker onto the arranged meat pieces on the platter and serve the smoky hot Corned Beef with Orange-spice.

21. Slow cooked Beef and Stout Casserole

This particular beef dish is famous in British pubs and this one is perfect if you need to whip up your dull mood. The special cooking process of the slow cooker makes the beef so velvety smooth that you will go mad for this and would want to have more and more. It's very satisfying, hearty meal that is irresistibly yummy. So, let's see the recipe of this rich, dark beef and stout casserole right away and plan to cook this over next weekend. You can serve over mashed potatoes or couple with rice and other vegetables or salad. It will taste divine always.

Preparation Time: 7 – 8 hours

Serves: 6 – 8

Ingredients:

- Beef (trimmed, cut into bite size pieces) = 3 pounds (1.4 kg)
- French Shallots (peeled) = 12
- Cup Mushrooms (small, trimmed) = 9 ounces (250 grams)
- Brown onion (coarsely chopped) = 1 large
- Bacon (cut into small pieces) = 6 ounce (175 grams)
- Garlic cloves (finely chopped) = 3
- Stout beer = 1 can of 15 ounce (440 ml)
- Beef broth or Campbell's Real beef stock = 13 ounce (430 ml)
- Fresh Thyme (chopped) = 2 tablespoons (9 grams)
- Tomato paste = 2 tablespoons (37.5 grams)
- Brown Sugar = 1 tablespoon (10 grams)
- Plain flour = 2 tablespoons (16 grams)
- Cold water = ¼ Cup (60 ml)
- Bay leaf = 1

- Pepper
- Salt

Let's Cook:

1. Take out your slow cooker. Combine all the vegetables along with thyme, pepper and salt in this. Top them with the meat pieces and bacon.
2. Whisk in the broth and stout beer onto the beef mixture in the cooker.
3. Close the lid, switch the cooker on and let it cook on low heat setting for 7 – 8 hours.
4. Once done, open the lid and discard the bay leaf.
5. Mix the flour with cold water in a small bowl. Pour this into the cooker on the beef mixture.
6. Turn the slow cooker heat setting to high and let it cook for about 30 minutes more or until desired thickness of the gravy is achieved.
7. Serve Beef and Stout Casserole hot and enjoy.

22. Beef and Carrot Ragout

Are you thinking about what to cook for dinner tonight? Here is a slow cooker comfort food, Beef and Carrot Ragout, which is supper easy to cook. Just get all the ingredients, do a little preparation and you are done. Your dinner will be served on time, smoky hot and you will simply love it. Once you have this, it is going to be a regular menu for your dinner as you won't get tired or bored of having it. It is such a delicious dish. So, are you ready to cook the yummy dish? Here we go.

Preparation Time: 4 – 5 hours

Serves: 4

Ingredients:

- Plain flour = ¼ Cup (32.5 grams)
- Gravy Beef (cut into bite size cubes) = 2.2 pounds (1 kg)
- Olive oil = ¼ Cup (56 grams)
- Brown onions (cut into wedges) = 2 large
- Garlic Cloves (crushed) = 2
- Tomato paste = ½ Cup (150 grams)
- Red wine = ½ Cup (125 ml)
- Campbell's Real Beef Stock = 1 Cup (250 ml)
- Thyme Sprigs = 3
- Carrots (large, peeled, coarsely chopped) = 3
- Pappardelle Pasta (cooked) (as needed for serving, optional)
- Pepper
- Salt

Let's Cook:

1. Put the plain flour in a zip-lock plastic bag. Also mix salt and pepper in this. Now add the beef pieces, lock the bag and shake it to coat the beef pieces with the flour nicely.
2. Take a large frying pan, heat the oil (1 tablespoon / 14 grams) in this over medium-high flame and brown the meat (half quantity at a time). Stir occasionally. Flip to each side and let it cook for at least 2 – 3 minutes on each side or until meats get nice brown color. Transfer all the browned meat pieces to your slow cooker.
3. Reduce the flame to medium and add the remaining oil in the frying pan. Add the onions and stir-fry until they are tender.
4. Now add garlic and tomato paste to the pan. Cook for another 1 minute. Now pour the red wine and bring to boil. Reduce the flame to low and keep the pan uncovered to let the wine get evaporated and come to half of its quantity. Add the beef stock, carrots and thymes. Let it come to boil. Pour this whole mixture on the browned meat in the slow cooker.
5. Close the lid, switch the cooker on and let it cook on low heat setting for 6 hours or on high heat setting for 4 hours.
6. Open the lid, sprinkle pepper and salt. Serve as it is or with cooked pasta.

23. Slow cooked Massaman Beef Curry

It's an exotic Thai delicacy that will be surely a great feast for your senses. The dish is rich, flavorful and scrumptious by all means. It has unique combination of Thai special spices. And as always slow cooking gives the beef a marvelously soft texture that it will melt in your mouth leaving a strong and long lasting flavor. You will relish this flavor of spices for long and will crave for more. Let's get the recipe for this Authentic Thai dish and get ready to have a blast.

Preparation Time: 8 – 9 hours

Serves: 4

Ingredients:

- Peanut oil = 1 tablespoon (14 grams)
- Beef Steak (trimmed, cut into bite size pieces) = 1.5 pounds (750 grams)
- Brown Onion (halved, thinly sliced) = 1 medium
- Curry paste Ayam Thai Massaman = ¼ Cup (56 grams)
- Garlic Cloves (crushed) = 2
- Cardamom pods (bruised) = 6
- Cinnamon Stick = 1
- Kaffir Lime leaves (vein removed, chopped) = 2
- Coconut milk = 1 can of 9 ounce (270 ml)
- Desiree Potatoes (peeled, thickly sliced) = 18 ounce (500 grams)
- Carrots (peeled, thickly sliced) = 2 large
- Fish Sauce = ¼ Cup (56 grams)
- Palm Sugar = 1 tablespoon (10 grams)
- Lime Juice = 1 tablespoon (15 ml)
- Steamed rice

- Peanuts (for serving)
- Coriander leaves (for serving)

Let's Cook:

1. Take a large frying pan, heat it over medium-high flame and put half of the oil in this. Brown the beef bites in batches. Cook all the meat pieces for 5 – 6 minutes each or until nicely browned. Transfer the meat pieces to the slow cooker you have.
2. Now heat remaining oil in the same pan. Add onion and keep frying by stirring occasionally until they become tender. Add garlic and the Massaman curry paste. Cook for 1 minute or until fragrances start coming out. Transfer this to the slow cooker as well.
3. Now add cardamom pods, cinnamon stick, coconut milk, lime leaves, potatoes, carrots, palm sugar and fish sauce to the cooker.
4. Close the lid, switch the cooker on and let it cook on low heat setting for 8 hours.
5. Once done, open the lid and discard cardamom and cinnamon. Add the lime juice to the cooked beef now.
6. Garnish with coriander leaves and peanuts. Serve as it is or with steamed rice.

24. Balsamic Pork Tenderloin

Now we will concentrate on a few pork recipes. This particular Balsamic pork tenderloin recipe will make you happy for sure. Because it demands only 5 minutes of your time for the preparation and you can leave the rest of the cooking process to your lovely slow cooker. And you will be happier to see and taste the outcome. It will be so outrageously sumptuous that you will just fall in love with your self-made delicacy. Here is the recipe for you.

Preparation Time: 6 – 6 ½ hours

Serves: 6 – 8

Ingredients:

- Pork tenderloin (boneless) = 2 – 3 pounds (908 – 1360 grams)
- Vegetable or chicken broth = 1 Cup (250 ml)
- Balsamic Vinegar = ½ Cup (104 grams)
- Worcestershire sauce = 1 tablespoon (14 grams)
- Soy sauce = 1 tablespoon (16 grams)
- Honey = 1 tablespoon (18 grams)
- Red Pepper Flakes = ½ teaspoon (1 gram)
- Garlic Cloves (chopped) = 2

Let's Cook:

1. Place the pork tenderloin at the bottom of your slow cooker.
2. In a small bowl, mix all other remaining ingredients. Pour this over the pork tenderloin in the slow cooker.

3. Close the lid, switch the cooker on and let it cook on low heat setting for 6 – 8 hours.
4. Once the cooking cycle is finished, open the lid and transfer the pork tenderloin to a plate. Tear it apart with two forks. Pour 1 cup of the gravy over this and serve.
5. If any extra gravy is left, store it in refrigerator for using in future.

25. Pork and Mushroom Ragout

If you need a break from regular meal menu, then this Italian pork dish is for you. You can cook this at home with your slow cooker and get a luscious treat in return. It is a rich, savory, flavorful and complete comfort food. It will make you feel like you are having your meal at any restaurant. That is the magic of the spices blended with pork and mushrooms. And slow cooking adds some extra deliciousness to the dish. So, make sure to cook this for weekend meal or whenever you expect guests at home. You will have blustery meal for sure.

Preparation Time: 3 – 4 hours

Serves: 2

Ingredients:

- Pork Tenderloin = ¾ pound (340 grams)
- Cornstarch = 1 tablespoon (8 gram)
- Tomatoes (crushed, canned, divided) = ¾ Cup (168 grams)
- Sun-dried tomatoes (packed without oil, chopped) = 1 tablespoon (3.5 grams)
- Dried Savory = ¼ teaspoon (0.3 gram)
- Fresh Mushrooms (sliced) = ½ Cups (37.5 grams)
- Onion (sliced) = 1/3 Cup (40 grams)
- Egg Noodles (hot cooked) = ½ Cup (75 grams)
- Black Pepper = 1/8 teaspoon (0.2 gram)
- Salt = 1/8 teaspoon (0.6 gram)

Let's Cook:

1. Rub the pork tenderloin with pepper and salt, nicely. Cut it in half.
2. Take a 1 ½ quart slow cooker; Arrange cornstarch, crushed tomatoes (1/2 Cup / 112 grams), sun dried tomatoes and dried savory in this.
3. Top it with pork, mushroom and onion. Pour remaining crushed tomatoes on this.
4. Close the lid, switch the cooker on and let it cook on low heat setting for 3 – 4 hours or until the pork is tender enough.
5. Meanwhile cook the egg noodles according to the instructions mentioned on its package and keep it aside.
6. Once the cooking cycle is finished, take out the meat onto a plate using a tong and cut into small slices with two forks or with a knife. Now pour the juice, left in the cooker, on these pork slices and serve with cooked egg noodles.

26. Country style pork tenderloin in gravy

It is one of the simplest roasted pork recipes one can cook with a slow cooker. Yet it is one of the tastiest pork dishes. It tastes best when served with mashed potatoes. The whole thing becomes so ambrosial that you will crave for this time and again. It will be a hit meal item for your entire family or whoever else tastes this. So, be worry free about what to cook for the next occasional party at home and win everyone's heart by cooking this awesome dish. The recipe is right here.

Preparation Time: 5 – 6 hours

Serves: 8

Ingredients:

- Whole pork loin roast (boneless) = 3 pounds (1.3 kg)
- All purpose flour = ½ Cup (65 grams)
- Onion powder = 1 teaspoon (2.4 grams)
- Mustard (ground) = 1 teaspoon (5 grams)
- Canola Oil = 2 tablespoons (28 grams)
- Low sodium chicken broth = 2 Cups (500 ml)
- Cornstarch = ¼ Cup (56 grams)
- Cold water = ¼ Cup (60 ml)
- Mashed Potatoes (optional)

Let's Cook:

1. Cut the roasted pork loin in half.
2. Put the all purpose flour into a zip-lock plastic bag. Add onion powder and ground mustard in this. Put the pork

pieces in it, zip-lock it and shake well to coat the meat pieces with flour mixture.
3. Now in a large skillet, heat the oil over medium-high heat and brown the meat pieces in this. Make sure all the sides of the pork loins get browned properly. Flip them over occasionally while browning.
4. Transfer the browned meat pieces to a 5 quart slow cooker.
5. Pour the chicken broth over the meat in the slow cooker.
6. Close the lid, switch the cooker on and let it cook on low heat setting for 5 – 6 hours or until pork is tender enough.
7. Once the cooking cycle is finished, remove the pork pieces with tongs and keep aside.
8. Remove and discard if there is any fat in the liquid, which is left in the slow cooker.
9. Take a large saucepan, pour 2 ½ Cups (750 ml) of the liquid onto this. In a cup, mix the cornstarch with cold water and pour this into the liquid in saucepan. Bring it to boil and keep cooking until desired thickness of the gravy is achieved. Once done, pour this gravy onto the pork pieces.
10. Serve this pork with gravy over mashed potatoes.

27. Slow cooked Pork Carnitas

'Carnitas' means 'little meat' and this particular 'Pork Carnitas' is a Mexican delicacy which was originated in a Mexican state called "Michoacan". If your taste buds are flexible in terms of tasting different flavors and are ready to check out internationally famous dishes, then you will surely enjoy this one. Once you taste this, you will just be obsessed with this dish. You can make it in form of Tacos, Quesadillas, enchiladas, Nachos, burritos and any other wrapping style. Moreover cooking this in slow cooker is super easy. So, you can consider this when you have less time for preparation and need to make quick and easy meal.

Preparation Time: 6 – 7 hours

Serves: 10 - 12

Ingredients:

- Pork Shoulder (bone-in, skinless) = 5 pounds (2.5 kg) or Pork Shoulder (boneless, skinless) = 4 pounds (2 kg)
- Onion (coarsely chopped) = 1
- Jalapeno (seeded, ribs removed, chopped) = 1
- Table salt = 1 ¼ tablespoon (5.5 grams) or kosher salt / sea salt flakes = 2 tablespoons (15 grams)
- Black pepper = 1 teaspoon (2.1 gram)
- Garlic Cloves (minced) = 4
- Juice from 2 oranges
- Dried oregano = 1 tablespoon (3.5 grams)
- Cumin (ground) = 2 teaspoons (4 grams)
- Olive oil = 1 tablespoon (14 grams)

Let's Cook:

1. Rinse and dry the pork shoulder and then rub it with salt and black pepper.
2. Again rub it with dried oregano, ground cumin and olive oil.
3. Now place the pork in the slow cooker with fat side up. Top it with onion, garlic, and jalapeno and squeeze the orange juice over this.
4. Close the lid, switch the cooker on and let it cook on low heat setting for 8 – 10 hours or on high heat setting for 6 hours.
5. The meat should be tender enough and should readily get separated from bone (if it was with bone). Remove the meat from the cooker and let it cool down a bit. Then shred it with two forks.
6. Skim the fat portion off from the liquid in the slow cooker.
7. Pour onto a saucepan and reduce / evaporate it over medium heat to attain a certain thickness. Keep aside.
8. Now heat 1 tablespoon (14 grams) of oil in another skillet over high flame and place the shredded meat in this. Press gently and keep cooking until all the meat pieces are golden brown in color and are crisp a bit.
9. Remove from heat and mix the shredded pork with the juice. This is now ready.
10. Wrap it in toasted tortillas or anything of your choice and serve immediately.

28. Slow cooked pork with Apple cider

The flavor of apple and pork goes so well that you can't imagine if you have never tasted this pork apple cider. And the way they complement each other is just amazing. We know slow-cooking makes any meat softer than normally cooked one. The apple cider here adds on to this and makes the pork extra soft and smooth. Cook this at home and you will know how much delicious is this pork preparation. Get the recipe now.

Preparation Time: 3 – 4 hours

Serves: 6

Ingredients:

- Olive Oil = 1 tablespoon (14 grams)
- Pork Neck Piece = 3.3 pounds (1.5 kg)
- Eschalots (peeled) = 12
- Fennel bulbs (thinly sliced) = 2 small
- Garlic Cloves (thinly sliced) = 3
- Apple Cider = Bottle of 12 ounce (355 ml)
- Chicken stock = 1 Cup 8.5 ounce (250 ml)
- Pink lady apples (cut into thick wedges, cored) = 3 large
- Fresh thyme leaves = 2 teaspoons (2.8 grams)
- Mashed potatoes (for serving)

Let's Cook:

1. Heat olive oil in a large skillet and brown the pork over medium-high heat. Flip over all sides while cooking.
2. Remove the pork from skillet and transfer to the slow cooker.

3. Add eschalots, fennel, bulbs, garlic, apple cider and chicken stock to the slow cooker.
4. Close the lid, switch the cooker on and let it cook on low heat setting for 3 – 3 ½ hours.
5. Add the apples now and cook for another half an hour. The apples should get tender by now.
6. Slice the pork pieces, sprinkle thyme leaves and serve with mashed potatoes.

29. Island Pork Roast

It is an amazing pork roast with a slight tangy and sweetish touch. It is a very simple yet complete comfort meal. When you are about to rush to office in the morning and have no clue about what to cook for dinner, consider cooking this dish. You can have it with rice, salad or any other side dish you like. In whatever way you have this, you will be assured to have a satisfying meal. The recipe is right here below:

Preparation Time: 5 – 6 hours

Serves: 10

Ingredients:

- Pork Loin Roast (boneless) = 1 (about 4 pounds / 1.8 kg)
- Pineapple Chunks (unsweetened, undrained) = 2 cans, each of 8 ounces (total 448 grams)
- Sugar = ½ Cup (100 grams)
- Lime Juice = ½ Cup (120 ml)
- Soy sauce = ½ Cup (116 grams)
- Brown Sugar (packed) = ¼ Cup (42 grams)
- Teriyaki Sauce = 2 tablespoons (20 grams)
- Garlic Cloves (minced) = 2
- Ginger (ground) = 1 teaspoon (1.8 grams)
- Curry Powder = 1 teaspoon (2 grams)
- Bay leaf = 1
- Cornstarch = ¼ Cup (32 grams)
- Cold water = ½ Cup (60 ml)
- Pepper = ¼ teaspoon (0.5 gram)
- Salt = ¼ teaspoon (1.25 grams)

Let's Cook:

1. Cut the pork roast in half.
2. Place the onions at the bottom of a 4 or 5 quart slow cooker. Then add the pork.
3. Drain the pineapple and reserve the juice. Keep the pineapple aside.
4. In a small bowl, mix sugar, lime juice, soy sauce, teriyaki sauce, brown sugar, ginger, garlic, curry powder, pepper, salt, bay leaf and reserved pineapple juice. Pour this mixture over the pork in the slow cooker.
5. Close the lid, switch the cooker on and let it cook on low heat setting for 5 – 6 hours.
6. Add the pineapple during the last hour of cooking cycle.
7. Once done, remove the pork, pineapple and onion. Keep them aside covered on a platter.
8. Discard bay leaf from the liquid in the cooker. Skim off fat from the liquid. Pour the liquid to a saucepan and bring to boil over medium-high heat. In another small bowl, mix the cornstarch with cold water. Stir this in to the boiling liquid. Keep cooking until desired thickness achieved.
9. Pour this sauce over the pork, onion and pineapple mixture.
10. The island pork roast is absolutely ready; Serve it warm (with rice, egg noodles or combo of veggies) and enjoy the dulcified dish.

30. Slow cooker Chicken Pot Roast

Here is a delectably simple slow cooker recipe that you can cook to have a perfect family breakfast, brunch, lunch or dinner. Roasted chicken is healthy obviously and when you cook this with slow cooker it becomes utmost yummy. In this dish, the chicken is roasted and seasoned perfectly to present you with a delightful feast of flavors and tastes. As this is an effortless dish to cook you can consider cooking it for a weekday dinner. Look at the recipe and gear up to cook.

Preparation Time: 8 – 9 hours

Serves: 6

Ingredients:

- Small potatoes (unpeeled, cut into 1 inch pieces) = 3 Cups (1 pound / 454 grams)
- Baby carrots (halved) = 2 Cups (492 grams)
- Small Whole onions (frozen, thawed) = 1 Cup (120 grams)
- Chicken Thighs (boneless, skinless) = 6
- Chicken Gravy = 1 jar of 12 ounce (350 ml)
- Sweet green peas (frozen, thawed) = 1 ½ Cups (215 grams)
- Black Pepper = 1/8 teaspoon (0.2)
- Salt = ½ teaspoon (2.5 grams)
- Non stick cooking spray

Let's Cook:

1. Take a 3 or 4 quart slow cooker. Apply the non stick cooking spray onto it to coat it evenly.
2. Combine potatoes, onions and carrots in the slow cooker.

3. Rub the chicken surface with salt and pepper. Place the chicken thighs in the cooker.
4. Pour the chicken gravy on this.
5. Close the lid, switch the cooker on and let it cook on low heat setting for 8 – 10 hours.
6. Turn the slow cooker heat setting to high, open the lid and stir in the thawed peas. Let it again cook for about 15 minutes or until the peas are softened.
7. The dish is now ready to serve. Just relish it.

31. Italian style Beef roast

This traditional Italian beef roast will make you fall in love with it once you taste it. Its spices give it tangy temptation which perfectly blends with richness of the beef and the final outcome is just heavenly. You can sense the soft texture of the beef as you have a bite. You will surely agree that you never had such a scrumptious beef dish. Just get the recipe and put your chef cap on to cook it. Make sure to cook good quantity, so you don't have to regret later when you will feel to have it more and more.

Preparation Time: 9 – 10 hours

Serves: 4

Ingredients:

- Beef Chuck pot roast (boneless) = 3 pounds (1.3 kg)
- Garlic Salt = 1 teaspoon (2 grams)
- Fennel seed (toasted, crushed) = 1 teaspoon (2 grams)
- Fennel bulbs (trimmed, cored, cut into thin wedges) = 2 medium
- Carrots (lengthwise halved, bias cut into thin slices or you can just cut them into cubes) = 3 medium
- Onion (cut into thin wedges) = 1 large (1 Cup / 120 grams)
- Pasta sauce = 1 jar of 26 ounce (728 grams)
- Penne Pasta (hot cooked) = 2 – 3 Cups (400 – 500 grams) or mashed potatoes
- Fresh Italian parsley (flat leaf, chopped) = ¼ Cup (6 grams)
- Grated Parmesan Cheese (optional)
- Black Pepper (ground) = ½ teaspoon (1 gram)
- Other veggies of your choice

Let's Cook:

1. Trim the fat portion off from the beef roast.
2. Take a small bowl, mix black pepper, fennel seed and garlic salt. Rub the beef chucks with this mixture.
3. Take a 5 - 6 quart slow cooker. Arrange fennel bulbs, carrots and onions in this. Place the roast on top of this layer. Pour the pasta sauce on it.
4. Close the lid, switch the cooker on and let it cook on low heat for 9 – 10 hours or on high heat for 4 ½ - 5 hours.
5. Toss the pasta or mashed potatoes with Italian parsley.
6. Top with grated cheese and serve the roast with pasta or mashed potatoes.

32. German style Beef roast with veggies

Beef roast seems to be loved by all and all continents have their own style of cooking beef roast. You can apply this recipe not only for beef roast but also for chicken and other meat types. This particular beef roast is a bit tangy and spicy. The beef is perfectly braised with wine and so lends a completely different taste. Everyone must cook and taste this zesty roast. Here is the recipe that will help you make this.

Preparation Time: 8 – 10 hours

Serves: 8

Ingredients:

- Beef Chuck pot roast (boneless) = 2 ½ - 3 pounds (1.1 – 1.3 kg)
- Cooking oil = 1 tablespoon (14 grams)
- Carrots (sliced) = 2 Cups (180 grams)
- Onion (chopped) = 2 Cups (240 grams)
- Celery (sliced) = 1 Cup (125 grams)
- Kosher style dill pickle (chopped) = ¾ Cup (127 grams)
- Beef broth or dry red wine = ½ Cup (125 ml) + 2 tablespoons (30 ml)
- German style mustard = 1/3 Cup (58 grams)
- Black pepper (coarsely ground) = ½ teaspoon (1 gram)
- Cloves (ground) = ¼ teaspoon (0.5 gram)
- Bay leaves = 2
- All purpose flour = 2 tablespoons (16 grams)
- Spaetzle or noodles (cooked)
- Fresh Parsley (snipped, optional)

- Other vegetables of your choice

Let's Cook:

1. Trim the fat portion off from the beef roast. Cut the roast into half.
2. Take a large skillet, brown the meat in this over medium-high flame. Make sure all the sides of the meat get browned evenly. Drain any extra fat.
3. Take a 3 ½ or 4 quart slow cooker. Arrange carrot, celery, onion and pickle in this. Place the meat on top of these vegetables in the cooker.
4. In a small bowl, mix red wine (1/2 Cup / 125 ml), pepper, mustard, bay leaves and cloves. Pour this over the vegetables and meat in the cooker.
5. Close the lid, switch the cooker on and let it cook on low heat setting for 8 – 10 hours or on high heat setting for 4 - 5 hours.
6. Once the cooking cycle is finished, remove the vegetables and meat from the cooker with a slotted spoon and transfer to a platter. Keep it covered so that it remains warm.
7. Discard bay leaves and drain off fat from the liquid in the cooker.
8. Take a saucepan, heat it over medium-high flame and transfer the cooking liquid from the cooker to it.
9. In another small bowl, mix flour and wine (2 tablespoons / 30 ml). Stir this into the liquid in the saucepan and bring it to boil. Keep cooking until gravy thickens a bit.
10. Serve the meat, vegetables and saucy gravy as it is or with noodles or rice.

33. Duck Ragu with Pappardelle

Here is a somewhat different slow cooker meat recipe. It's a duck recipe. Are you curious? Let's see the recipe to know more. Apart from duck, this particular dish has Pappardelle pasta noodles that are very large, broad and flat type. This combination of duck and pasta noodles along with variety of spices and vegetables makes this dish a really special and unique. Once you start eating this, you will know how divine it tastes. You will never get bored having this.

Preparation Time: 4 – 5 hours

Serves: 6

Ingredients:

- Duck (frozen, thawed) = 4 pounds (1.8 kg)
- Pancetta (sliced, coarsely chopped) = 3.5 ounce (100 grams)
- Brown onion (finely chopped) = 1 small
- Celery stick (finely chopped) = 1 small
- Carrot (peeled, finely chopped) = 1 small
- Garlic cloves (finely chopped) = 2
- Bay leaves (dried) = 2
- Pinot noir = 1 Cup (250 ml)
- Tomatoes (diced) = 2 cans, each of 14 ounce (total 800 grams)
- Chicken stock = 1 Cup (250 ml)
- Rosemary springs (fresh) = 3 large
- Chinese five spice = ¼ teaspoon (1 gram)
- Pitted Green Olives (finely chopped) = 2/3 Cup (110 grams)
- Pappardelle Pasta (cooked, for serving)
- Grated parmesan cheese (for serving)

- Fresh continental parsley (finely chopped, for serving)

Let's Cook:

1. Cut either side of the duck backbone with a kitchen scissor. Discard the backbone. Trim off extra fat portion. Cut the whole duck into quarter. Brown the duck on a large skillet over medium-high heat. Again drain off any extra fat and transfer the browned meat to a slow cooker.
2. Add all ingredients to the cooker except pasta, cheese and parsley.
3. Close the lid, switch the cooker on and let it cook on low heat setting for 4 – 5 hours.
4. Once the cooking cycle is finished, the duck is transferred to a platter and kept covered.
5. Transfer the liquid from slow cooker to a saucepan and keep it boiling until the liquid reduces to 1/3 rd amount.
6. Shred the duck meat with two forks and pour the thick liquid over this.
7. Sprinkle grated parmesan cheese and parsley on the dish and serve along with Pappardelle pasta.

34. Nachos with Shredded Beef

These shredded beef nachos are perfect as weekend meal. You can enjoy this Mexican dish with your family or with your friend in an outdoor weekend party. It can be eaten in any season and at any time. They taste divine always. Once you taste this you would want to have it every weekend and any time in the middle of the week also. They look, feel and taste so yummy that nobody can ignore these Nachos. Making and keeping the shredded beef filling ready for dinner or having these nachos as dinner is a fantastic idea. So, let's take a look at the recipe now.

Preparation Time: 6 – 8 hours

Serves: 8 - 12

Ingredients:

- Chili powder = 2 teaspoons (5.6 grams)
- Cumin (ground) = 1 teaspoon (2 grams)
- Paprika = ½ teaspoon (1 gram)
- Garlic Cloves (crushed) = 3
- Round or chuck steak = 3.3 pounds (1.5 kg)
- Chicken stock = 1 Cup (250 ml)
- Olive oil = 2 teaspoon (5 grams)
- Onion (finely diced) = 1 small
- Corn chips = 2 bags, each of 6 ounce / 175 grams (total 350 grams)
- Grated cheese = 2 cups (160 grams)
- Sour cream = 1 Cup (250 grams)
- Black pepper = 1 teaspoon (2.1 grams)
- Salt = 1 teaspoon (5 grams)

- Avocado = 2 medium
- Lime (juiced) = 1 large
- Any other veggies for topping as per your choice

For salsa:

- Tomatoes (diced) = 3 medium
- Red onion (diced) = ½ medium
- Garlic Clove (finely chopped) = ½
- Olive oil = 1 tablespoon (14 grams)
- Coriander (chopped) = 2 tablespoons (6 grams)

Let's Cook:

1. Take a small bowl; combine chili powder, cumin, paprika, pepper and salt. First rub the garlic on the meat surface and then rub this spice mixture nicely.
2. Place the meat in the slow cooker and pour the chicken stock over this.
3. Close the lid, switch the cooker on and let it cook on low heat setting for 6 – 8 hours or on high heat setting for 4 - 6 hours.
4. Meat should be tender enough and fall apart from bone easily by now. Remove the meat from the cooker and shred with two forks.
5. Heat the oil in a frying pan, cook onion for couple of minutes, add the beef and stir fry for couple of minutes more. Pour the left over cooking liquid into this and cook for another 2 – 4 minutes.
6. Mash the avocadoes; mix with lime juice and Keep aside.

7. Mix together all the salsa ingredients and season well. Keep aside.
8. Pre-heat your oven to 220°C (428°F). Line a large baking tray with baking paper. Layer half of the corn chips. Sprinkle half of the grated cheese and layer half of the shredded beef. Repeat the same sequence one more time. Bake for 10 minutes till the cheese gets fully melted.
9. Transfer the whole thing from baking tray to a serving platter. Serve with avocado mixture, sour cream and salsa.

35. Greek Lamb with Orzo

It is a great one pot meal option to cook in slow cooker when you really have less time for preparation. Just you have to get the ingredients and rest all will be done by the slow cooker. It is a kind of lamb roast that is cooked with herbs and served with orzo, a special type of small pasta that looks like rice grain. Let's see the recipe and you will know how easy it is to make at home.

Preparation Time: 8 – 9 hours

Serves: 6

Ingredients:

- Lamb shoulder (bone-in, cubed) = 2.2 pounds (1 kg)
- Onion (sliced) = 2
- Fresh oregano = 1 tablespoon (3 grams) or dried oregano = 1 teaspoon (1 gram)
- Cinnamon stick (snapped in half) = 2
- Cinnamon (ground) = ½ teaspoon (1.2 grams)
- Olive oil
- Tomatoes (chopped, canned) = 14 ounce (400 grams)
- Vegetable, chicken or lamb stock (hot) = 2 pints (944 ml)
- Orzo pasta = 14 ounce (400 grams)
- Parmesan cheese (for serving)

Let's Cook:

1. Take a large saucepan, heat the olive oil in this over medium-high flame and brown the lamb cubes. Flip them over occasionally to make sure all the sides of the meat get browned properly.

2. Combine all the remaining ingredients in your slow cooker except orzo and parmesan cheese. Stir to mix well.
3. Close the lid, switch the cooker on and let it cook on low heat setting for 8 – 9 hours or on high heat setting for 4 - 5 hours.
4. When last half an hour of the cooking cycle is left, open the lid, discard the cinnamon sticks and stir in the orzo pasta. Close the lid and let it complete the cooking cycle. Peek in the slow cooker to see whether orzo has absorbed all the liquid or not. If it looks too dry, then you can add (50 ml) some water in this.
5. Once done, sprinkle grated parmesan cheese over this and serve hot.

36. Beef and Bean Tortilla

This layered beef and bean tortilla is a very easy-to-make dish and it tastes just outstanding. Anyone can go mad for it once tasted. You can even try it with different meat like turkey breasts and also experiment with other ingredients. And you will be amazed to see that every time the outcome will be so astonishing. So, what is stopping you? Put your gloves, apron, chef cap and whatever else you like on and get ready to cook this. The recipe is right here for you.

Preparation Time: 4 – 5 hours

Serves: 4

Ingredients:

- Beef (ground) = 1 pound (454 grams)
- Onion (chopped) = 1 small
- Black Beans (rinsed, drained) = 1 can of 15 ounces (420 grams)
- Tomatoes (diced) and green chilies (sliced) = 1 can of 10 ounces (280 grams)
- Ripe Olives (sliced, drained) = 1 can of 2 ¼ ounces (70 grams)
- Chili Powder = 1 ½ teaspoons (4 grams)
- Hot pepper sauce = 3 drops (1 ml)
- Flour tortillas (8 inches) = 4
- Cheddar Cheese (shredded) = 1 Cup (4 ounces /112 grams)
- Fresh Cilantro (minced, optional)
- Black Pepper = 1/8 teaspoon (0.2 gram)
- Salt = ½ teaspoon (2.5 grams)

- Non stick cooking spray
- Heavy duty aluminum foil

For salsa (optional):

- Sour cream
- Lettuce (shredded)
- Tomatoes (chopped)

Let's Cook:

1. Take 20 x 3 inch heavy duty aluminum foil strip and place at the bottom of a 5 quart slow cooker. Apply the non stick cooking spray to coat the lining evenly.
2. Take a large skillet; Add meat and onion together. Cook for a while until the pinkness of the meat goes away. Drain and keep aside.
3. In the same skillet, add beans, tomatoes, chili powder, olives, pepper, salt and hot pepper sauce. Stir fry for couple of minutes. Lastly add the meat again and mix well. Put one cup of this mixture at the bottom of the slow cooker. Place one tortilla on this and then spread ¼ cups (28 grams) of cheese. Repeat the layers 3 times.
4. Close the lid, switch the cooker on and let it cook on low heat setting for 4 – 5 hours.
5. Using the sides of foil lining as handles, remove the whole tortilla stack out of the cooker and place on a platter.
6. Mix all salsa ingredients together in a bowl.
7. Sprinkle cilantro on it. Serve with salsa if you wish.
8. Cut the stack into quarters before serving.

37. Shredded Beef Barbeque

The prominent flavor of shredded and spiced beef is the center of attraction for this dish. It is so rich in flavor and taste yet so easy to make that you will become fan of this recipe once you try this. You can serve this as a burger filling or with coleslaw or with just a bun. You will enjoy the dish in any way. Its good as a quick meal and you can pack this in box while rushing for office. Making this for a crowd also is a good idea; just make in good quantity. Quality of the dish will any way win the hearts of your guests. You can try it at any time. Just get the recipe here.

Preparation Time: 6 – 7 hours

Serves: 12

Ingredients:

- Celery salt = 1 teaspoon (5 grams)
- Garlic powder = 1 teaspoon (2.1 grams)
- Onion powder = 1 teaspoon (2.1 grams)
- Beef brisket (fresh) = 1 (2 -3 pounds / 1.1 – 1.3 kg)
- Liquid smoke (optional) = 3 tablespoons (45 ml)
- Hot pepper sauce = 1 tablespoon (10 grams)
- Barbeque sauce = 1 bottle of 18 ounces (504 grams)
- Sandwich rolls (split) = 12

Let's Cook:

1. Combine celery salts, onion powder and garlic powder in a small bowl. Rub this mixture on the meat.

2. Now place the meat in a 5 quart slow cooker. Pour the liquid smoke and hot pepper sauce on this.
3. Close the lid, switch the cooker on and let it cook on low heat setting for 6 – 8 hours or until the meat is tender enough.
4. Once the cooking cycle is finished, open the lid, remove the meat and let it cool down a bit.
5. Keep only about ½ Cup (125 ml) of the cooking liquid. Discard the extra liquid from the cooker. Whisk in barbeque sauce into this liquid.
6. Shred the meat with two forks and put it back into the cooker. Mix well. Again heat it thoroughly.
7. Take out 1/3 Cup (80 grams) of the mixture and put on each roll and fold them. It is not absolutely ready to serve.

38. Slow cooked Beef Stroganoff with crunchy onion

This is recipe from heaven for the beef lovers. It is renowned Russian delicacy that is adored worldwide. This particular beef stroganoff has crunchy onion to complement its zesty appearance. You can serve it with rice, egg noodles or just as a single dish. It tastes and feels vibrant in all combinations. It's a great dish for a winter outdoor get together. The recipe is jotted down in details below.

Preparation Time: 4 – 5 hours

Serves: 8

Ingredients:

- Beef Chuck Stew Meat (cut into 1 ½ inch cubes) = 3 pounds (1.3 kg)
- Golden mushroom soup = 2 cans, each of 10 ¾ ounce (total 645 ml)
- Mushrooms (sliced) = 1 package of 8 ounce (224 grams)
- French Fried onion = 2 cups (4 ounce / 112 grams)
- Classic Worcestershire sauce (low sodium) = 1/3 Cup (56 grams)
- Water = ¾ Cup (175 ml)
- Pepper
- Salt
- Cooking oil = 2 tablespoons (28 grams)

Let's Cook:

1. Rub the meat with salt and pepper to season well.

2. Take a large saucepan. Heat the oil over medium-high heat and brown the meat. Flipping over couple of times will make sure that all sides of meat are browned properly.
3. Take a 5 quart slow cooker. Transfer the browned meat into this.
4. Stir in mushroom soup, sliced mushrooms and 1 cup (55 grams) of French Fried Onions into the slow cooker. Also add Worcestershire sauce and water to it. Mix well.
5. Close the lid, switch the cooker on and let it cook on low heat setting for 8 hours or on high heat setting for 4 hours or until the meat is tender enough.
6. Sprinkle remaining 1 cup (55 grams) of French Fried onions over the cooked meat.
7. Serve it hot with rice or noodles.

39. Smoky Beef Brisket Tacos with Shredded Cabbage

Many people love smoky beef tacos. And slow cooked beef tastes awesome always. So, with a slow cooker handy, you have no reason to worry about the taste of the final dish. You can blindly say that any Crock-pot cooked meat would taste divine, no matter what the ingredients are and how you have arranged everything. And this one is also no exception. The cabbage topping is a special twist to this preparation. So, you can try this beef dish without any second thought and be sure to have a blast while having your meal.

Preparation Time: 8 hours

Serves: 4 - 6

Ingredients:

- Beef Brisket = 4 pounds (1.8 kg)
- Smoked Paprika = 1 teaspoon (2.1 gram)
- Cumin (ground) = 1 teaspoon (2 gram)
- Onion powder = 1 teaspoon (2.1 gram)
- Chili powder = ½ teaspoon (1.3 grams)
- Beer (any brand of your choice) = 8 ounces (240 ml)
- Red Cabbage (shredded) = ½
- Limes (juiced) = 2 + extra for serving
- Olive oil = 1 teaspoon 5 grams)
- Sweet corn (optional) = 2 ears
- Queso Fresco Cheese (crumbled) = 4 ounces (112 grams)
- Flour tortillas = 8 – 10
- Pepper = 1 teaspoon (2.1 grams)
- Salt = 1 teaspoon (5 grams)

Let's Cook:

1. Take a small bowl; combine salt, pepper, paprika, cumin, onion powder and chili powder. Rub this mixture on the beef brisket to season well.
2. Place the seasoned beef brisket in the slow cooker. Pour the beer on this.
3. Close the lid, switch the cooker on and let it cook on low heat setting for 8 hours.
4. Once the cooking cycle is finished, take the brisket out of the slow cooker and place on a cutting board.
5. With the help of a knife and a fork, shred the brisket. Put the shredded meat back to the slow cooker, add lime juice, toss it and let it cook for another half an hour. Meanwhile also toss the meat couple of times.
6. Take another bowl; put the shredded cabbage and toss with lime juice, olive oil, salt and pepper. Add the beef into this bowl; Mix nicely.
7. Place spoonful of this mixture on the tortillas. Also add spoonful of sweet corn and crumbled cheese with this.
8. Finish assembling the Tacos and serve warm.

40. Asian Beef curry

Asian dishes are famous for their aromatic spices, rich colorful look and tempting taste. This particular Asian beef curry tastes best when eaten along with steamed rice. It is a completely comfort food that will keep your tummy full and happy for hours. It is best as day meal. The rich and spicy gravy along with raw broccoli will give you feel of diving treat. You will never get bored having this dish over and over again. So, trying to cook this dish with your great slow cooker is must. You can adjust the spice levels while cooking according to your preference and that will not affect the taste of the outcome. The recipe is right here.

Preparation Time: 6 – 8 hours

Serves: 4

Ingredients:

- Top round or bottom round beef roast (boneless) = 3 – 4 pounds (1.3 = 1.8 kg)
- Chicken broth or beef broth = 1 Cup (250 ml)
- Balsamic Vinegar = ½ Cup (100 grams)
- Honey = ¼ Cup (75 grams) + 2 tablespoons (36 grams)
- Soy sauce = 1 tablespoon (16 grams)
- Fish Sauce = 1 tablespoon (15 grams)
- Asian Chili-garlic sauce = 1 -2 tablespoons (15 – 30 grams) or according to taste or desired level of spiciness
- Garlic Cloves (peeled, lightly smashed) = 4 – 6
- 1 piece of ginger (2 inch, lightly smashed)

Let's Cook:

1. Place the beef roast in the slow cooker. Scatter or sprinkle the garlic and ginger all over the meat. Stir in broth, balsamic vinegar, honey (1/4 Cup / 75 grams), soy sauce and fish sauce. Also add Asian chili-garlic sauce at the last.
2. Close the lid, switch the cooker on and let it cook on low heat setting for 6 – 8 hours or on high heat setting for 4 hours or until the beef is tender enough.
3. Take out the beef from the slow cooker and place on a platter. Let it cool down a bit.
4. Transfer the cooking liquid from the slow cooker to a saucepan. Heat it over medium-high flame. Add the remaining honey (2 tablespoons / 36 grams) and bring it to boil. Keep boiling and let it reduce to its ¾th quantity. The more you reduce it, the more flavors it will generate.
5. Now shred the beef with two forks as thinly as possible.
6. Pour the boiled sauce over the shredded beef and toss it.
7. It is now ready. Serve it with stir-fried broccoli and steamed rice. Your meal is going to be a pleasant one for sure.

41. Slow cooked Round Steak

Here is another yummy beef preparation. Try this at home during holidays or at any time you feel you need to make a quick and easy meal. It is super simple recipe but yields a very zesty and tempting outcome. This saucy beef dish goes well with mashed potatoes or rice or stir-fried veggies or cream or noodles. It also tastes equally divine when eaten single. So, just get the recipe and try it. You will love it.

Preparation Time: 7 – 8 hours

Serves: 6 – 8

Ingredients:

- All purpose flour = ¼ Cup (32 grams)
- Beef round steak (boneless, cut into bite size pieces) = 2 pounds (908 grams)
- Canola oil (divided) = 6 teaspoons (28 grams)
- Onion (medium, thinly sliced) = 1
- Condensed cream of mushroom soup (undiluted) = 1 can of 10 ¾ ounces (322 ml)
- Dried Oregano = ½ teaspoon (1 gram)
- Dried Thyme = ¼ teaspoon (0.3 grams)
- Black Pepper = 1/8 teaspoon (0.2 gram)
- Salt = ½ teaspoon (2.5 grams)

Let's Cook:

1. Take a zip-lock plastic bag, put the flour into it and also add salt and pepper. Add the beef round steak pieces into it and

shake well to coat the meat pieces well with flour. Put a few pieces of meat at a time. Repeat the process for all meat pieces.
2. Take a large skillet, heat it over medium-high flame, add canola oil and brown the meat pieces, few at a time. Flip them around to make sure all the sides get browned properly.
3. Transfer the browned meat pieces to a 5 quart slow cooker.
4. In the same skillet, stir-fry onion in the left over oil until they become opaque.
5. Put the stir-fried onion on the meat pieces in the slow cooker.
6. In a bowl, mix mushroom soup, thyme and oregano. Pour this mixture over meat and onion in the cooker.
7. Close the lid, switch the cooker on and let it cook on low heat setting for 7 – 8 hours.
8. Once done, serve it with any side dish and toppings of your choice.

42. Balsamic Glaze Roasted Beef Tenderloin

When whole beef tenderloin is cooked with Balsamic Glaze in slow cooker with perfection it yields wonderful treat. I bet you never had such an elegant and satisfying beef preparation. As a matter of fact, slow cooker or crock-pot is known to make any dish utmost delicious. So, you can be worry free if you have one at home. The whole cooking concept becomes so easy, that you won't hesitate to cook any dish under the sun. So, you can try this beef recipe at any time and with full confidence. Christmas eve party or any other occasion will be nice time to try this super tasty dish. Here is the recipe for this.

Preparation Time: 4 – 5 hours

Serves: 8

Ingredients:

- Beef Tenderloin (10 inch long, preferably the thick end of a whole tenderloin) = 3 – 4 pounds (1.3 – 1.8 kg)
- Thick Pepper Bacon = 12 strips
- Onion (thinly sliced) = 1 small
- Garlic Cloves (peeled) = 4
- Fresh Rosemary Sprigs = 3 – 4
- Beef Stock = ¾ Cup (185 ml)
- Balsamic Vinegar = 1/3 Cup (70 grams)
- Dijon Mustard = 1 tablespoon (15 grams)
- Sugar = 2 tablespoons (25 grams)
- Flour =1 tablespoon (8 grams)
- Pepper (as needed)
- Salt (as needed)

Let's Cook:

1. Rub pepper and salt on the beef tenderloin surface thoroughly.
2. Place the bacon strips on a clean work surface, slightly overlapping each other and create a rectangular shaped sheet of bacon.
3. Lay the whole tenderloin on the bacon sheet and wrap with the end of bacon strips over the top. Secure the loose end with toothpicks and attaching two ends together.
4. Take a large skillet, heat it over medium-high heat and place the whole tenderloin wrapped with bacon sheet (with toothpick side down) in this. Turn the bacon on all sides every 10 minutes. Flip it over to make sure all the sides of bacon get browned properly. You can perform this step ahead in advance and refrigerate the whole thing for 1 – 2 days and take it out whenever you wish to cook the dish.
5. Take a 5 – 6 quart slow cooker and place the tenderloin wrapped with bacon sheet in this. Don't forget to pour the pan drippings over it.
6. Place the onion slices on the meat, also scatter garlic cloves and rosemary sprigs around it.
7. If possible, insert an oven safe meat thermometer into the thickest part of the tenderloin.
8. Close the lid, switch the cooker on and let it cook on low heat setting (thermometer should read 130°F) for 2 – 4 hours.
9. Mix the flour and sugar in a small bowl. Stir in balsamic vinegar and mustard into it. Mix well to make sure there are no lumps. Also add beef stock in this and mix again.

10. Reduce the heat even more and let the temperature come to 100°F. Then open the lid, pour the flour mixture onto the meat, cover and continue to cook till the temperature again reaches 130°F.
11. At this time, open the lid, remove the tenderloin and keep wrapped in foil for 10 minutes. Let the cooker run till 135°F temperature arrives. The gravy in the cooker should be thick enough by now. The Balsamic Glaze is ready.
12. For serving remove the toothpicks and cut the tenderloin into slices. Top it with Balsamic Glaze and serve.

43. Thit heo kho tieu

Here is a treat for the Chinese food lovers. This pork recipe has touch of Asian aromatic spices and also lots of veggies. The name 'Thit heo kho tieu' in Chinese means 'five-spice caramel pork'. It is completely healthy, comforting and satisfying dish. It is good source of energy and you can be sure about your low calorie intake. The flavorful dish does not demand much of your time for preparation. It is pretty simple to cook. The recipe explained below will help you to cook this dish flawlessly.

Preparation Time: 6 – 7 hours

Serves: 8

Ingredients:

- Peanut oil = 1 tablespoon (14 grams)
- Pork belly (cut into bite size pieces) = 2.2 pounds (1 kg)
- Asian purple eschalots (finely chopped) = 8
- Garlic Cloves (crushed) = 2
- Light soy sauce = ¼ Cup (60 ml)
- Palm sugar (finely chopped) = ¾ Cup (125 grams)
- Water = 1 cup (250 ml)
- Star Anise = 2 whole
- Chinese Five spice = 1 teaspoon (5 grams)
- Fish sauce = 1 tablespoon (15 grams)
- Green Shallots (ends trimmed, diagonally cut into thin slices) = 8
- Steamed rice (may be Sunrise Jasmine Fragrant one or any other of your choice, for serving)
- Lebanese Cucumber (ends trimmed, thinly sliced) (optional)

- Fresh coriander leaves (optional) = ½ Cup (15 grams)

Let's Cook:

1. Heat the peanut oil in a skillet and brown the meat pieces thoroughly. Do this in batches if needed depending on the size of your skillet. Transfer the browned pork pieces to your slow cooker.
2. Add eschalots, garlic, soy sauce, palm sugar, water, star anise and 'Chinese five spice' into the slow cooker.
3. Close the lid, switch the cooker on and let it cook on low heat setting for 6 – 6 ½ hours.
4. When last 30 minutes of the cooking cycle is left, add the fish sauce and half of the shallot to the cooker and turn the heat setting to high.
5. Once done, transfer the whole pork preparation from slow cooker to a serving platter and top with remaining shallots, cucumber and coriander leaves. Serve the yummy dish with steamed rice and enjoy the meal.

44. Slow Cooker Mediterranean beef roast

This is a simple yet flavorful and zesty Mediterranean delicacy that promises to steal your heart with its magic. Beef roast is nothing new. However, the combination of beef with other ingredients here is unique and that lends a special flavor to the dish. It's a must try dish for a busy week day. The recipe is in details below.

Preparation Time: 6 – 7 hours

Serves: 8

Ingredients:

- Beef chuck roast (boneless) = 3 pounds (1.3 kg)
- Italian seasoning = 1 tablespoon (4.5 grams)
- Garlic Clove (finely chopped) = 1 large
- Sun-dried tomatoes in oil (drained, chopped) = 1/3 Cup (18 grams)
- Kalamata olives (ripe, sliced, pitted) = ½ Cup (90 grams)
- Beef flavored Stock (preferably Progresso) = ½ Cup (from a 32 ounce / 960 ml carton)
- Pearl onion (frozen) = ½ Cup (from 1 pound / 454 grams bag)
- Non stick cooking spray

Let's Cook:

1. Apply the non stick cooking spray to a 12 inch large skillet.
2. Book the beef in skillet until brown. Flip them around in every 5 minutes to make sure all the sides of the meat get browned properly.

3. Sprinkle salt, Italian seasoning and garlic on the meat. Now remove the skillet from the heat.
4. Take a 4 or 5 quart slow cooker. Place the browned beef in this. Scatter the sun-dried tomatoes and olives all over this. Add onions and broth.
5. Close the lid, switch the cooker on and let it cook on low heat setting for 5 – 6 hours or until the beef is tender enough.
6. Once the cooking cycle is finished, open the lid and remove the beef from the cooker. Keep it aside covered and let it cool a bit. Slice or shred the beef with knife or forks.
7. Pour the cooking liquid from the slow cooker onto the beef and serve hot.

45. Slow cooker Beef Au jus

'Au jus' is a French term which means 'with juice'. That simply indicates that this dish is zesty, luscious and juicy one. It is quite easy to cook. It has very few and easily available ingredients. All it demands is a little time for preparation, time for serving and finally eating. That's it. The cooking part is totally hassle free and will be taken care by your slow cooker. So, just peek at the recipe, gather the ingredients and get ready to cook. Be assured to have a blast at meal time. Mostly this beef preparation is served as sandwiches or clubbed with two pieces of any bread. However, you can do some variations with the side dish, like you can serve this with stir-fried baby carrots and boiled potatoes or whatever else you like. It would be a good idea to cook this when you expect pretty big group as your guest.

Preparation Time: 6 – 7 hours

Serves: 10

Ingredients:

- Beef bottom round roast or rump roast = 1
- Onion (large, sliced) = 1
- Low sodium beef broth = ¾ Cup (185 ml)
- Au Jus Gravy mix = 1 ounce (28 grams) or 1 envelope ()
- Garlic Cloves (halved) = 2
- Pepper – ¼ teaspoon (0.5 gram)
- Salt (if needed)
- Non stick cooking spray

Let's Cook:

1. Cut the beef roast in half.
2. Take a large skillet and apply the non stick cooking spray on it.
3. Put the beef pieces, may be one at a time depending on how large is your skillet, cook over medium-high flame until they turn brown. Flip them around in every 5 minutes to make sure all the sides of the meat get browned properly.
4. Take a 5 quart slow cooker. Place the onion in this. Then add the browned meat pieces.
5. In a bowl, mix beef broth, garlic, pepper, salt and gravy mix. Pour this onto the meat in the slow cooker.
6. Close the lid, switch the cooker on and let it cook on low heat setting for 6 – 7 hours or until the beef is tender enough.
7. Once the cooking cycle is finished, open the lid, remove the beef and place on a cutting board. Let it stand for 10 minutes. Then thinly slice the beef with knife and put them back to the slow cooker. Mix well.
8. Beef Au Jus is ready. Serve with any side dish or breads or just as it is. It will taste awesome in any way.

46. Pork and beef meatballs with Rigatoni Pasta

This could be the richest meat recipe you have ever had. It has pork and beef and that too combined with yummy pasta. The tempting combo of cheesy pasta with meat can't be ignored. Although it sounds to be too many items to cook for a single dish, in reality it is pretty quick and easy slow cooker recipe. It is totally hassle free and you can cook this casually on a weekday or over weekend. Needless to say, this can be a hit item for a grand party. So, consider cooking this whenever you have party at home next time. For now, just peek at the recipe.

Preparation Time: 6 – 7 hours

Serves: 4

Ingredients:

- Pork and beef Mince = 26 ounce (750 grams)
- Pecorino Cheese (finely grated) = 1/3 Cup (80 grams) + more for serving
- Garlic Cloves (crushed) = 3
- Fresh Parsley (flat leaf, finely chopped) = 2 tablespoons (3 grams)
- Fresh Breadcrumbs = ¼ Cup (33 grams)
- Olive oil – 1 tablespoon (14 grams)
- Brown onion (chopped) = 1 medium
- Celery stalks (chopped) = 2
- Dry Sherry = 1 tablespoons (15 ml)
- Tomato paste = 18 ounce (500 grams)
- Caster Sugar = 2 teaspoons (8 grams)
- Rigatoni Pasta = 12 ounce (350 grams)

- Cold water = 6 Cups (1.4 liter)

Let's Cook:

1. Mix meat mince, garlic, cheese, parsley, and breadcrumbs in a bowl. Take tablespoon full of mixture and shape as ball.
2. Heat oil in a medium sauce pan, add onion and celery. Stir fry for 4 – 5 minutes. Add sherry and cook for another couple of minutes. Stir in tomato paste, sugar and water. Transfer this mixture to a 5 quart slow cooker.
3. Add the meatballs in the cooker.
4. Close the lid, switch the cooker on and let it cook on low heat setting for 6 hours or until the meatballs are tender enough.
5. Add the pasta, and again cook for about 45 minutes or until the pasta is cooked and sauce is thick enough. Season by sprinkling salt and pepper.
6. Serve Pork and beef meatballs with Rigatoni Pasta right away.

Printed in Great Britain
by Amazon